La Folie Forty

Thierry Tellier and Jennifer Jones

Baer Books Press

Chicago   Hattingen

$\mathcal{B}aer\ \mathcal{B}ooks\ \mathcal{P}ress$

Published by Baer Books Press

Chicago | Hattingen
baerbookspress.com

Published in the United States of America
by Baer Books Press

This edition published 2015

Copyright @ 2015 by Thierry Tellier and Jennifer Jones

Library of Congress Control Number: 2015956910

La Folie Forty / Thierry Tellier and Jennifer Jones

ISBN-10: 0991326865
ISBN-13: 978-0-9913268-6-0

http://www.baerbookspress.com/
Designed by Denise Baer • *Cover Art by Denise Baer*

DEDICATION

For Franck, Aurore, and Danielle. You have been the most important part of my *La Folie* Forty. And in honor of the memory of my grandparents who taught me respect for food and for hard work. ~Thierry Tellier

For the memory of my grandmother, Hilda Maxwell, who never once complained about this young girl child's early attempts at "cooking." ~Jennifer Jones

TABLE OF CONTENTS

"Find something you're passionate about and keep tremendously interested in it."
~Julia Child

"Here with a Loaf of Bread beneath the Bough,
    A Flask of Wine, a Book of Verse - and Thou
    Beside me singing in the Wilderness –
    And Wilderness is Paradise enow."
~Omar Khayyam

Du pain du vin et Peuple Sera Saint.

"We write to taste life twice, in the moment and in retrospect."
~Anaïs Nin

A Note From Jennifer Jones

This beautiful book will delight your senses and tempt your taste buds. It will interweave Thierry Tellier's love of food, his love of life, and his love of family. It will also showcase his life story—his *la folie* forty—through the course of the forty stories that follow this introduction. However, I have one story of my own to share first—if you don't mind pausing to read it.

Life's journey simply amazes me, sometimes. Does it you? Many of us frequent small American towns—like Blacksburg, VA—or even neighborhood *cafés*—such as Our Daily Bread—in either our daily lives or in our travels. We usually do so completely encompassed within our own individual bubbles. We are so engrossed in the present that we simply float along without a thought about the future or what interactions may lay just around the bend.

Then, a random action causes us to collide with another bubble. As each of our little bubbles go POP, our feet touch the ground, and we stand astounded as we look back to where we began, embrace where we are, and look forward to the fascinating journey that lies ahead. The following is how my own tiny bubble bumped into Thierry Tellier's one sunny March day.

◆◆◆

My once fiancé, now husband, moved from city life in Ohio to Southwestern Virginia in late January of 2015. Shortly thereafter, he not only married me, but also found employment in a local *café* and bakery—Our Daily Bread. I had eaten at the *café* many times down through the years, but had only caught a glimpse of the man behind the delicious food, Thierry Tellier. I had no personal knowledge of him. But that was soon to change.

Working the breakfast shift every morning, my husband got to know his boss on a more personal level. One day in particular, Thierry mentioned in conversation that he had so many stories from his days in the bakery and restaurant business that he should write a book. It was on his "bucket list" to view his life's story in book form. However, he needed someone to actually write it, as he was only comfortable in speaking the English language—not writing it.

My husband promptly spoke, "My wife is a writer." Thierry reflected for a moment, and then expressed interest in an introduction. Later that afternoon, upon arriving home, my husband mentioned his conversation from earlier that morning. He asked if the thought of such a project held any appeal. I was both surprised and, admittedly, a bit nervous. I had never attempted such an endeavor into the nonfiction world. Fiction writing and poetry had always been my go-to's. But naturally, both my writer's curiosity and excitement of possibility replaced the nerves in record time.

I was introduced to Thierry Tellier less than a week later. The ice broke quickly. Soon, we were plotting and creatively planning. On April 3, 2015, barely over a week after our initial meeting, I navigated toward Thierry's house armed with that same writer's curiosity, an empty notebook, and a handful of pens.

Over the course of the spring and summer, the cherry tree in Thierry's backyard bloomed and faded, verdance, vegetables, and flowers—many flowers—carpeted the yard, and that once empty notebook became filled with details. Those details evolved into stories, and those stories—along with treasured family photos and prized recipes—soon comprised this book that you now hold. One random conversation between an employee and his boss catalyzed the whole creative endeavor. Simply amazing.

◆◆◆

I thank you for taking the time to read my story, but now it is time for you to immerse yourself in Thierry Tellier's. It is my sincerest hope that—both through my words and his recipes—you experience Thierry's voice loud and clear throughout it all. Happy reading!

Prologue

In France, where I am from, we treat dining as fine art. Our ingredients are likened to the highest quality of paints, cooking implementations are our brushes, and the palate is our canvas. Imagine if you will, the earthy, intoxicating fragrance and the verdant greens of fresh herbs. Or the snap of a grape's skin in your mouth after you have just pulled it from the vine and the fruit's cool, sweet burst as it caresses your tongue.

Imagine knowing that such leafy treasures will be dried for market and the fruit will be miraculously transformed into a beverage that lingers on your palate with notes both crisp and complex. Imagine cheese soft and creamy as you dip in your fingertip, with the perfect mildness and hint of salt. Or imagine bread—firm, golden and crusty—its scent as tantalizing to your nose as that of any perfume. Food for us isn't merely meant for sustenance—it is a feast for the senses.

I have been a part of creating such delights, such art, for forty years and wow, what a forty years it has been. Simply put, this life of mine has been crazy, thus the name of this book *La Folie* Forty—crazy forty. The pace, the hours, and the intensity—only someone labeled as crazy would have been willing to do what I have done for so long. But, I will admit it, I *am* crazy. Crazy from the joy of cuisine. And I would not take back a single moment. If anything, I am proud of and humbled by the life that I have led thus far—so much so that I wish to share it all with you.

As you traverse the following pages, I hope that you will find yourself transported back in time to my youth in my native France. You may be surprised to find it very similar to your own, or it may be quite different. Either way, I think that you will be able to relate and perhaps learn a few new facts, as well.

The Loire Valley, where I was raised, is as rich in history as it is in harvest. We will not delve into the back-story of my country's royalty and how they transformed the valley—that can be saved for another publication much different than mine. But you will bear witness to my own bygone days—various snapshots in time and moments in my life—through the stories that I will share. You will read about the people who have touched my life, both in large ways and in small ways. Some of their names might differ from reality, to protect their anonymity, but the heart of who they are is embedded upon the following pages.

Most importantly, may you grow to treasure the dishes that are woven into the tapestry of each of these moments in my life as much as I do. These dishes are as much a part of me as my own skin and bone. Most of them are simple—some of them are more complex, but all of them are satisfying and reproducible. And may they inspire you to create stories of your own—through life and through food. Thank you for taking this journey along with me back into my past. *Savourez*—enjoy!

~Thierry Tellier

Bread In My Veins

Mom holding me

Dad holding me

Most children of my generation were born at home. As for me, I was born in a bakery. The scent of cooling croissants, particles of flour hanging in the air like motes of dust suspended in a lazy afternoon sunbeam, the feel of that same talcum flour on a butcher block counter as I brush my fingertips across it, the taste of fresh-from-the-oven crust melting onto my tongue—this is home to me.

Down through the years, my existence and bread have always been intertwined. A life such as this is all that I have ever known. I am convinced that as I grew inside of my mother, the scent of my father's baking bread permeated her womb, yeast bloomed within my veins, and dough stretched to form my marrow.

I did not choose this life for myself. It became mine, all the same. My parents purchased and established seven bakeries, as well as three carts, over the course of my life with them. I worked side by side with them in all but one— the one in which I was born. It burned before I had the chance, as I was only about two years old then.

They only baked bread in this first bakery, and rustic brown bread, at that. That was all that my father knew back then. This style of bread was the staple of our region. During this time, bakeries were unlike the ones that exist today, such as my own Our Daily Bread. Back then, very few sales were made in the actual bakery. Typically, the wife—for instance, my mother—would deliver bread from farm to farm, similar to the way that milk was delivered from door to door.

My parents had a small, commercial car—a Renault Juvaquatre, what we called a Juva4—which my mother used for such deliveries. Oftentimes, they traded, or bartered their delicious, aromatic bread for food items that my family required for sustenance. The act of this bartering put more than just bread on our own table at mealtimes. My parents ran this bakery for approximately two years until, as I previously noted, it suddenly and catastrophically burnt.

I was sent to live with my grandparents after the bakery fire, which I greatly enjoyed, as most any grandchild would.

My sister lived with other relatives. My parents were not keepers of great wealth, and after the fire's destruction of their only source of income, what little money they possessed did not stretch very far. After we were sent away, my father searched for another bakery. He took on the position of realtor to provide for him and my mother during his search, because he had a good head for business. This position also aided in his quest.

Eventually, my father's search culminated with yet another bakery, and my sister and I rejoined my parents on a full-time basis. There is no question—even though I was born in the first bakery, my actual life—both the good and the bad of it—began in the new village that housed my family's second bakery. It is there that I learned the art of bread. It is there that I learned the beginnings of the art of living.

Bread has been, and continues to be, my life. Not only was I born in a bakery, I grew in a bakery. I evolved in a bakery. And I am still progressing in, yes, a bakery.

DAD'S BROWN BREAD

Ingredients:
- 3 lbs. flour
- 1 oz. salt
- 3/4 tbs. dry instant yeast
- 1 lbs. "bread water" ←
- 2 lbs., 9 oz bread flour

8 oz. stale wheat bread, broken into bread crumbs (fine to slightly chunky) combined w/ 10 oz. water in a bowl (room temperature). Cover bowl in plastic wrap w/ holes poked in it; let sit out overnight at 70° (at least 18 hours).

Directions:

1. After you've made your bread water, mix all ingredients at a slow speed until combined. (~3 min.) Then adjust to a higher speed and mix for another 6-8 minutes, until dough reaches 76° F. Form a relatively firm ball of dough on the hook of your mixer.

2. Remove the dough from the hook and place it in a greased bowl covered with plastic wrap or paper towel. Let sit for 2 hours at 70-75° F (dough itself should be 76°F). During this time, at about halfway through, fold the dough once.

3. Divide the dough into 1.5 lbs. portions. Shape into bâtards (a loaf similar to a baguette, but shorter and wider). Place them on a baker's cloth or paper towel, cover in plastic wrap, and refrigerate overnight — no more than 12 hours.

4. Bake at 460° F in a steamed oven for 20 minutes or until dark brown with a hard crust.

My Father's Hands

Dad on bike outside the bakery

My father was an enigma. He was as multi-faceted as any diamond. The portion of his personality that he decided to reveal to you depended on his mood, his relationship with the person, or how much he had imbibed that day. Anywhere we went, though, the townspeople adored him. To them, he was a handsome man—dark haired, stocky, and strong, with an easy smile and a carefree laugh. In his younger days, those qualities made all the girls swoon, or so I was told.

An apprentice baker's trade, not just another average farm boy's, was all that it took to win my mother's heart. And it didn't hurt that he roamed the French countryside to visit her on his "dangerous" motorcycle. Mother, a pale, refined blonde, was quite beautiful, herself. They made quite the handsome pair and wed in 1955. After their union, my father discovered his first bakery—my birthplace. It was located in a village approximately 30 kilometers from my mother's village.

He purchased this bakery, and he and my mother moved into the living quarters above it. Nine months later,

I was born, and eighteen months after that, my sister arrived. I was told that my parents devoted their sweat, energy, and the labor of their hands to this bakery. It thrived, accordingly—until it burned.

As a boy, what impressed me the most about my father was the size of his hands. They were huge! To a small child, such as myself, they were borrowed from a giant. But, with time, the size of his hands made perfect sense to me.

As I grew, I learned that one had to be strong to be a baker, and large hands were quite useful. Flour was packaged much differently back then. An average sack of flour weighed one hundred kilos, or around two hundred pounds, and my father's powerful hands could lift such a weight with ease. Can you imagine such sacks lining the shelves of your local grocery store today?

My father was certainly a complex man. I could reveal many things about him, some of these being good, and some not so much. But one thing that I will say with complete conviction is that he was an excellent baker. He knew flour. He knew bread. And with time, he kneaded me into his likeness.

As a young boy, I never cared for the bread making in the bakery. Perhaps this was simply a preference of mine, or because the work was time consuming and sometimes difficult, or perhaps it was because of my relationship with my father. But I can still smell the hint of sweetness in the air—the delicate aroma of my father's genius transformed into loaves of *brioche*. I still smell them because currently they line the shelves of my own bakery. His recipe has become my own.

BRIOCHE

ingredients:

8 oz. milk	3 lbs. bread flour
1½ lbs. eggs	7 oz. sugar
1 tbs. lemon zest	1 oz. salt
1½ lbs. cold butter	1 oz. instant dry yeast

directions:

1. combine all ingredients with a paddle on medium-high speed. Mix for 8-10 minutes or until dough lifts from side of the bowl.
2. Pull dough off paddle and place back into the bowl. Add the butter and mix for another 10-12 minutes, or until butter has absorbed.
3. Place dough in a greased bowl and cover with plastic wrap. Let sit for 45 minutes.
4. Fold dough once, then re-cover the bowl and refrigerate overnight (at least 12 hours).
5. Remove dough from fridge. Cut into 1-pound portions, and place into molds. Coat with egg wash and sprinkle with brown sugar.
6. Bake at 340°F for 26-30 minutes or until golden brown.

1 egg + 2 tbs. water (beaten)

No. 3
To Grandmother's House We Go

What I remember the most about my grandparent's house is the pigs. You see, my grandparents resided in a country village roughly three hundred kilometers from Paris. The Loire Valley, where their village was located, was famous for its wine, and this attracted droves of royalty. The valley's lush landscape, dark, fertile soil, and

My grandparents

rolling hills were dotted with castles and estates belonging to the French nobility and elite. It was like a medieval version of the suburbs.

My grandparents' village was home to the castle of a rather infamous Madame. The Madame was the niece of a certain prominent writer, well to do, and reclusive, since her husband had passed away in World War I. Because of these facts, throughout the village, gossip regarding her spread thicker than my grandmother's homemade butter. My grandparents did not pay attention to such gossip and chose, instead, to work hard to provide sustenance for themselves, my mother, and my aunts.

They leased the land surrounding her castle, farmed the property, and raised herbs, vegetables, an abundance of beautiful flowers, chickens—for the meat as well as for the fresh eggs—and, my favorite, pigs! While we feasted every day on the bounty, the carrots, leeks, turnips, rutabaga, and collard greens, along with apples and pears, would also be sold at market. I would accompany my grandparents every Thursday to the market where they would both sell their wares and purchase family necessities, such as flour. My grandmother weighed everything on her own scale before she took it to market, and this scale was passed down to me. It is a cherished memento from those days of my youth.

But at the time, I ignored the rest of the farm. It was the pigs that fascinated me. If you recall, I was but a tiny boy when my mother and father's bakery burned to the ground, and I was sent to live with my grandparents until further arrangements could be made for the family. My favorite thing to do at Grand-mère's was to stand on the gate, grip the edge tightly, and peek over the top to spy on the pigs. Standing on my toes, I could barely view them, and my grandmother would often shoo me away. But I would sneak back to see them every chance that I could muster. I learned not to grow too attached to the pigs, however, as they were not pets, but served a much higher purpose— Grand-père's breakfast.

My grandmother would cut the pigs in half lengthwise, hang them, and then finish curing them with salt. Next, she would cook them in her wood-burning oven, cover them to keep the flies at bay, and serve them cold. Ahhh, even today the memory of the hearty scent from that pork roasting in the oven makes my mouth water. Grand-père and I enjoyed the fruits of her labor every morning—with a side of oven-roasted potatoes.

Grand-mère used her wood-burning oven to occasionally bake bread for the family, as well. I mostly savored her handmade butter. The salt and cream burst in my mouth. I would often dip my little fingers into the butter dish when she wasn't looking. Once I became old enough to understand them, I heard stories about the German occupation of the village and how her oven was used to bake bread during WWII. My grandfather was adamant about not sharing war stories, as he had been held captive as a prisoner of war in the 1st World War. Such stories brought back too many tragic memories for his liking.

I imagine that my life during this time period had paralleled that of my mother's in her youth. It certainly brought me great joy. Sadly though—to the dismay of all grandchildren at some point in their lives or another— visits with the grandparents eventually come to an end.

After my father discovered our second bakery and he called to reunite our family, the new village to which we relocated was close to Chinon, Tours, and Vouvray, and quite far away from my grandparents—well over one hundred kilometers. I saw them much less after the relocation. But I have always remembered that time in my life with substantial fondness. And I will never forget those pigs!

Salted Pork and Potatoes

ingredients:
3 lbs. skinless pork belly
½ cup kosher salt
3 tbs. sugar
1 gallon chicken broth
6 tbs. olive oil, divided
2.5 lbs. Yukon gold potatoes, quartered
3 tbs. sugar

directions:
1. Combine salt and sugar, then rub them over the pork belly. Wrap it in plastic and refrigerate overnight, or up to 12 hours.
2. Preheat oven to 350°F, rinse the pork, and pat it dry with paper towels. (Use a pot just wide and deep enough to hold the pork covered fully in broth.) Sear the pork on medium heat with 3 tbs. of olive oil until it is a deep golden brown on both sides.
3. Pour out all excess oil from the pot, cover the pork with the chicken broth, return it to the stove, and bring to a boil over high heat.
4. Cover and place in the oven for one hour and a half. Check with a fork or knife for tenderness. If not, cook additional time, checking every 20 minutes or so, until tender.
5. Remove pork from oven and raise temperature to 400°. Let pork rest. Once it is cool enough to handle, remove it from the broth. Cut it in half lengthwise, then into one inch thick strips. Transfer to a plate and hold until serving.
6. Place the potatoes in the reserved broth and cook them in the oven until tender. Serve with the pork.

No. 4
Brothers and Sisters

Me & Sis

As a young boy, I ran around with two dirty, grubby best friends, I adored my dog, and I disliked my sister. My friends and I were dreamers with our heads lodged somewhere in the clouds. At times, we could be quite rotten. The local birds and rats could attest to this. We rode our bikes over every square inch of our village, played with marbles and slingshots, foraged in the woods, and made boats that we sailed on our favorite pond.

Now, don't get me wrong—I loved my sister. We just shared a typical relationship that most siblings do during this age range. To a young boy and his friends, my sister was mostly annoying. I made it well known that I wanted to play with my friends and not with her, but she still followed me closer than my own shadow did.

She would challenge us to bicycle races, even though she knew that we were faster and stronger. She would then attempt to chase us on her own bicycle, would inevitably fall, and cry some more. This gave us—the jubilant victors—time to escape. We knew we had to use the time wisely, because somehow she always caught up to us.

My father adored my sister. She made good marks in school and was sweet to him. I did not spend much time in school, because my assistance was required at the bakery. Even so, schoolwork did not come easily to me. My marks showed as much, however running the bakery consumed my parents' time and energy, so they paid little mind. My sister loved to show off her knowledge and culture, and my response was usually rolling my eyes and finding creative ways to compete with her.

One such competition—and my favorite one, at that—was held daily at the breakfast table. We ate *baguettes* and drank *café au lait* every morning for breakfast. My sister and I would scarf down as many of these as possible—as quickly as possible. We would even compete to see who could dunk our crusty bread first into our steaming cups of coffee. It was a joy to start off my day matched head to head against her in a challenge that I could—and often did—win!

I looked forward to breakfast the way most children look forward to Christmas. Every night, before bed, my mother would mix water, ground coffee, and chicory in the coffeepot and allow it to steep on the stovetop overnight. Coffee was rather expensive back then, and chicory root was readily available in our area. Mixing the two of these together stretched the coffee—and our budget—further. And what a delicious combination!

In the morning, my mother would pour creamy milk into the hot liquid, and I would watch as the dark and the light swirled together in my cup. The chicory added an earthy depth to the mixture, and its presence, along with that of the freshly ground coffee, danced across the palate of even a young boy such as me. Eventually, when I was much older, I skipped the coffee altogether and only drank the brewed chicory and milk. I was that enamored with its flavor.

To pair such a drink with crusty, flaky *baguettes* and salty, creamy, hand-whipped butter was simply divine. In this region of France, the people had always eaten simple brown bread like my father was accustomed to baking. White "French" bread as is well known today was not made. That is, until the day our commercial mixer broke.

My father was quite the mechanic, and he and his

friend, both tipsy from the village *café's* libations, decided to fix the mixer. They tore it all apart—parts littered the bakery floor in a jumbled heap. To my surprise, they pieced it back together. In doing so, the belts that ran the mixer were shortened and thus moved at a faster pace. This allowed more air to be dispersed into the dough, and, accordingly, the *baguette* was finally served in our area.

My sister and I were indeed most grateful for this mix-up. It was one of the only things that we ever agreed upon.

Café au lait

ingredients:
4 ½ cups milk
4 ½ cups fresh espresso
brewed ground chicory, to taste

directions:
In a medium pan over low heat, heat the milk until bubbles form around the edges. Whisk to form frothy bubbles. Add the espresso and ground chicory. Serve and enjoy!

baguette

ingredients:

3 1/2 cups water
1.25 oz. salt
1/2 tbsp. instant yeast
1 lbs. firm leaven — pre-ferment
2 lbs, 7 oz. bread flour

directions:

1. combine all ingredients and mix on slow speed for 3 minutes. mix for another 8 minutes on medium-high speed until dough reaches 76° F. let sit for 2 hours, folding halfway through.

2. Divide the dough into 11 oz. pieces and shape them into baguettes. Place on towels and refrigerate overnight, about 12 hours.

3. Remove from fridge and let dough return to room temperature. Score each baguette with a sharp kitchen knife. Remove from the towels and bake at 420° F in a steamed oven for about 18 minutes or until brown.

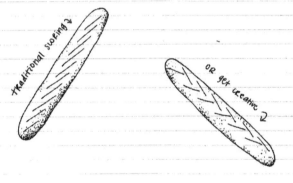

Traditional scoring →

or get creative →

No. 5
Mother's Sunday Chicken

My Parents

For some families, Sundays were reserved for rest and relaxation—but not for our family. They were the busiest days of our weeks. On Sunday mornings, I rose early for prep work with my mother—so she could deliver bread by truck later in the day—and, after that, church. Then it was back to the bakery for lunch and more work.

Finally, by late afternoon, there was enough time for me to be able to enjoy my surroundings for a bit. My friends were typically right there beside me for playtime. We knew better than to play too loudly or close to home, for fear of disturbing my father. I learned that lesson myself all too well after experiencing flour thrown in my face, amongst other forms of discipline. So we would usually go exploring around the pond in the woods. To three spirited boys, our little corner of the world seemed so large. I discovered though, years later when I returned as an adult, that it was indeed quite small.

On Sundays, my family ate lunch around 1 to 2 pm. It was a treat to be able to consume a meal other than breakfast so early in the day. During the week, we typically ate dinner after 8 pm, because we had to wait for the bakery to close. This was the only other meal that time afforded us after breakfast, as we were too busy on normal weekdays to break for lunch.

My father insisted on eating some form of meat every night with dinner. Otherwise my mother's dishes were not that remarkable to me. We certainly never went hungry, but we ate food merely to survive, not to savor. I would learn to do this once I had grown up. That being said, I will never forget the scent of her Sunday chicken wafting through the bakery.

My mother wasn't nearly as talented with day-to-day cooking as other mothers in the village. But her chicken would bring me running every week! She prepared the chicken early in the morning with butter and herbs and cooked it in our wood-burning oven while we were at church. The fresh herbs seasoned the bird with a snap of flavor. The chicken's taste took on the profile of whichever herbs she decided to use that day.

Rubbing the poultry's exterior with butter allowed its skin to become crisp and brown, while its interior remained moist and tender. Never dry, my mother would pull it from the oven with perfect timing. The juices would linger on my fingers and then on my tongue. Some rubbed the chicken down with oil rather than with butter, but my mother always claimed that the butter was key to bringing out the flavor of the chicken. *C'est vrai*—it is true.

To this day, my wife occasionally cooks this dish for me on Sundays, and even now, the scent of it takes me back to those days in my youth.

Mom's Chicken & Herbs

Ingredients:

1 4-lbs chicken

4 oz butter

salt & pepper

fresh herbes de Provence

3 ea. shallots

1 head garlic

directions:

1. Rub entire chicken with butter - season with salt and pepper, and sprinkle herbs over top.
2. slice shallots. separate garlic and crush it. stuff mixture into cavity of chicken.
3. preheat oven to 350° F. leave chicken at room temperature for one hour before cooking.
4. cook at 350° F for one hour. take chicken out and make sure the juices run clear. let sit 15 minutes before serving.

No. 6
First Love

In the first decade of my life, I fell in love with the doctor's daughter, or so I thought. I "loved" her, but I did not like her. She was much too pretty, and the saying proved true: beauty can only be skin deep. I thought I knew about love, but actual true love would touch my heart a bit later in my life—in my twenties, when I met the woman who would become my wife.

My Parents

At such a youthful age, perhaps I did not know as much as I thought I did about love. But I did become embroiled in quite a love affair—a love affair with pastries. I came to know them quite intimately. And such *amour* has grown along the span of my life, continuing even today.

At our second bakery, my parents—specifically, my mother—were introduced to pastry making. It was *bon chance*—good fortune—both a happy, and delicious, circumstance. An army pastry chef had discovered our bakery as he was passing through our village. He petitioned my father for means of temporary employment. This gentleman was quite skilled in pastries. His sweet treats were works of art, and my mother and I became dazzled by them, as we had never seen such delicacies in a bakery setting. Up until that time, all that we had known was bread.

The pastry chef passed his knowledge on to my mother, who was a quick study. My father left this learning to her capable hands as he was mostly disinterested and chose, rather, to stick with the making of the bread. The gentleman left our bakery rather quickly, as we knew that he would. He was simply passing through our small village on his way to new adventures. But after he left, my mother continued on with her newfound talent.

She used quality ingredients, and the tantalizing scents of her *chouquette* and *croquembouche* warred with those of my father's brioche and croissants for sensory domination. Her *croquembouche*—towers of light, flaky balls of dough coated with sugary sweet drizzled caramel—were both a culinary delight and a beauty to behold. They were so lovely, in fact, that it was almost painful to witness them being torn apart for consumption. That is, until your fingers were coated with delectable caramel. Then, the guilt passed and the savoring began.

The *chouquette* were similar to the American cream puff. They were made with exactly the same dough as the *croquembouche*. These pastry balls would be laid out individually on a tray and coated with sugar or a sweet, delicate cream. Villagers would come to the bakery to purchase these and my mother always gave them their choice of topping. The *chouquette* was, and still is, my favorite. In my young mind, these treats lined the streets in heaven. In fact, they are still sold on the streets of Paris today. What a sweet tradition.

I can still remember the joy that I felt as I licked the sugar and cream off of my fingers. The taste of my mother's pastry dough lingered in my mouth long after my last bite. And thus, a life-long love affair was born.

Croquembouche

choux:

ingredients:
1 lbs. water	.7 oz. salt
1 lbs. milk	2 lbs. flour
1 lbs. butter	~20 eggs
.7 oz. sugar	

1. In a pot over medium heat, combine the water, milk, butter, sugar, and salt. Heat until butter is melted and the mixture starts to bubble around the edges.
2. Add the flour and stir over the flame with a wooden spoon, until a ball of wet dough forms. Continue stirring until all of the excess moisture on the dough is gone.
3. Transfer the dough into a bowl. Stir until it's no longer hot. Add the eggs one by one, mixing in each one individually. Continue adding eggs until the dough reaches a consistency at which it could fall off the spoon like a ribbon — not too thick or thin. Drier dough will ~~be~~ require more eggs.
4. Using a piping bag, pipe the dough into 1.5" balls on ~~preheated above~~ a cookie sheet lined with parchment paper, or directly onto a lightly greased non-stick pan.
5. Bake at 365° F for 25-30 minutes or until golden brown.

creme patissiere:

ingredients:
1 lbs. milk	.25 ~~lbs.~~ lbs. egg yolks
.25 oz butter	.6 lbs. sugar
1 vanilla bean	

1. Combine the milk and half of the sugar with the vanilla bean. Bring to a boil.
2. In a separate bowl, combine the rest of the sugar with the egg yolks, whisking energetically until the color pales and the texture becomes fluffy.
3. Add 1/4 of the boiled milk into the sugar/egg whip. Whisk them together, then ~~add~~ pour the entire mixture into the pot with the milk. Whisk until it returns to a boil, then continue whisking for another 2 minutes. The consistency should be a thick, creamy custard.
4. Remove from stove. Cut the butter into cubes then add them to the pot, whisking until fully combined. Wrap with plastic wrap, making sure the plastic is directly against the custard — no air. This is to prevent a film from forming. Put it in the freezer until cold, but not frozen.
5. Re-whip the custard after removing it from the freezer. Add the Grand Marnier (1-2 oz. per pound).
6. Poke the flat part of the choux with the tip of the piping bag, and fill each one with the creme patissiere.

Caramel:

Ingredients:
1 lbs. sugar
.25 lbs. water

Boil until desired consistency at 320°F. Dunk pot in cold water to prevent overcooking.

assembly:

Dip the tops of the choux halfway into the caramel, then stick face down onto parchment paper or silicone pad. Arrange the base in a circle, filling it in with choux. using the caramel as a paste, continue building the croquembouche in the form of a conical tower.

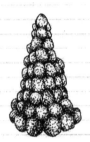

Saturday Night "Specials"

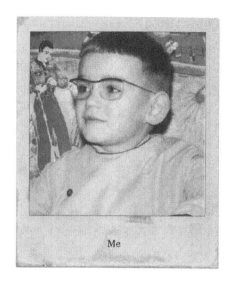

Me

Growing up, I dreaded Saturdays the way most people would dread a visit to the dentist. Saturday was the day that the bread pans needed cleaning, and guess who was always assigned that chore? You guessed it—me. Ugh! I could never jump in early in the day to complete the job, either. Saturday morning was like every other morning— busy. Trust me, those pans saw their fair share of use on that day. So I would be forced to wait until afternoon, inwardly moaning and groaning the whole time.

My father was particular when it came to cleanliness, and cleaning the pans took away anywhere from two to four hours of my afternoon, depending on if one particular friend of mine would help me or not. This friend took pity on me most Saturdays. Plus, he knew that the sooner the job was completed, the sooner we could sneak away to play with our marbles. My other friend was not so benevolent with his time. He would always wait for us to finish the chore before he came around. Smart boy.

After the pans were finished, my mother would close down the bakery for the day and prepare our evening meal. While she did this, my friends and I could play, although it was short-lived. After our family finished dinner, we had to begin making the *croissants*. The thought of it made me groan just as much as having to clean the pans did!

I hated helping with the *croissants* because it was a difficult, time-consuming process. The dough had to be flattened paper thin and of an even consistency. Thank goodness that my father had a hand *laminoir* to aid in the task. He was the first in the area to own such a device, and it was a blessing not to have to roll out the dough by hand. It would have taken twice as long.

The dough was inserted into one end of the *laminoir* and as the handle was cranked, it came out the other side much flatter and more even. However, even with the machine's assistance, it was still an aggravating endeavor. The dough's consistency had to be almost perfect to meet my father's standards. After this undertaking was finally completed, the flattened dough was then left to proof overnight.

Those buttery, flaky, melt in your mouth *croissants* were popular in the village, and integral to the bakery's business. Needless to say, much dough had to be prepared for the week, as we only had the time and opportunity to work such dough on Saturday evenings. My father's *croissants* were delicious—I will not lie. In fact, I still use his recipe, yet for a young boy, their preparation was soul draining.

There was a highlight to the toil of my Saturday nights, though. Eliot Ness and The Untouchables. I could not get enough of that show! We were fortunate to own a tiny, black and white television set, and it was located downstairs in the bakery. I could watch bits and pieces of the show as long as I kept up with my work. My friends and I were thrilled by the escapades of Eliot Ness. The Untouchables was a constant in our weekday conversations: "Did you watch it? Wow! Can you believe what happened? Did you see it when...?" We waited every week with bated breath for a new episode. Yes, we were addicted!

Actually, there were two highlights to my Saturday nights. The second was the making of the Baguette Viennoise. These *baguettes* were unique, and similar to the croissants, were typically made on Saturday night. Ah, but the making of these brought me such pleasure. Unlike our other *baguettes*, these were made with sweet milk. Their flavor was light and delicate as it settled upon your tongue.

After the dough was prepared, it was placed in a mold that held seven *baguettes* per tray. The tops were then scored with a special blade in a diagonal fashion. The baking process would turn the design of the baguette into a thing of true beauty. Once that dough came into contact with the oven's heat, and its rope-like crust browned—perfection! The Baguette Viennoise could easily and deliciously stand on its own, but when it is used in French bread pudding, as my wife and her family love to do, it becomes more decadent—if that is possible!

Heart-racing entertainment and beautiful bread—these Saturday night specials saved a young boy from weekend nights of drudgery, *certainement!*

baguette viennoise

ingredients:

1 lbs. flour
2 oz. salt
1 oz. fresh yeast
1 oz. milk powder
4 oz. soft butter
10-12 oz. cold water
pinch of salt

directions:

1. Combine all ingredients except butter. Mix for 8-10 minutes on second speed.
2. Add butter and continue mixing until completely combined.
3. Cover the dough with towels for 45 minutes.
4. Cut 5-lbs. pieces of dough, and roll them like small baguettes. Coat with egg wash (from Brioche recipe). Make cuts on the bread like the diagram — these baguettes are scored many times.
5. Let proof for 45 minutes - 1 hour. Bake at 350° F for 20-25 minutes.
6. Serve with salted butter.

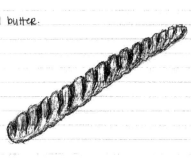

No. 8
Happy Accident

Quite early into my mother's pastry making days, her business began to boom. The villagers could not get enough of her sweet treats, and neither could I! My mother was an enterprising woman in her own right, and she took it upon herself to introduce the people to her delicacies—even those who did not frequent the actual bakery. She accomplished this by way of Sunday deliveries.

Mom

As I have mentioned many times over, bakery life was not a life of leisure. With my mother's newly found talents, time for inactivity became even less likely. On Sunday mornings, we would now rise at five a.m. to prepare fruit tarts to sell on her delivery run, and on these days, I would commonly skip church to accompany her. I was older then, and I did not particularly care for the village priest, so I did not mind.

Even though she was a beginner, my mother's tarts were exquisite. The crust was flaky, rustic, and perfectly browned. The interior of that crust housed a delectable custard cream base with a topping of lightly seasoned fresh fruit, like peaches, apples, or pears—when these were in season. Otherwise, we relied on canned fruit when fresh fruit was not as plentiful.

Although I had to rise early to provide assistance, I particularly enjoyed fashioning these pastries. Of course, I also held a special affinity for my mother. Her pastry making inspired the very first creation by my own hands. I would sneak dough from my father, employ the techniques that my mother used, cook my specialties in the oven when my father wasn't paying close attention, and share these sweet treats with my friends

After we moved to our current village, and the bakery business began to thrive, we ceased delivering bread in our tiny Juva4. Instead we employed the use of a Renault Estafette. The interior of this larger van style of truck was

Me

outfitted with at least three baskets to carry bread, and a shelf to hold my mother's tarts. She would park the Estafette, slide back its side door, and *voila*—instant access to the bakery's wares. It was, in essence, an ancestor to the modern day food truck.

One particular Sunday morning, while we were out delivering, my mother and another gentleman—we will call him Guillaume—collided in a minor car accident. After the commotion from the accident died down, my mother and Guillaume became more properly introduced. When he learned that my mother was in fact the baker's wife, his eyes gleamed, and in short time, so did mine. This man generated food for the army, and he was in desperate need of bread. This bread was to be shipped out to men in need by way of the nearby Air Force airstrip. The airstrip was located just outside of the village, and to my friends and me, it represented both possibility as well as unknown lands. It wowed us!

Guillaume struck up a deal with my father to provide 2,500-3,000 *petit pans*—or tiny, three to four inch *baguettes*—per day to the Army. This was a lot of dough, both literally and figuratively! The contract turned into quite the lucrative deal for my parents and even further established their bakery within the community. And, thankfully, my father owned the proper commercial equipment to be able to make these. Could you imagine mass-producing that many *baguettes* by hand?

Guillaume became a good friend to my family, and to me, as you will see later. I discovered that he was quite the excellent cook. Into my teenage years, he became my mentor. Under his supervision, I truly began to appreciate and savor food, and I learned about life in the process. Who knew that a simple car accident and my mother's fruit tarts would eventually take me there?

FRUIT TART

ingredients:
1 lbs. all-purpose flour
½ lbs. powdered sugar
.4 lbs butter
3 eggs
vanilla (optional)

directions:
1. use a paddle mixer to combine flour, sugar, and butter until they create a sandy-textured mixture.
2. Add the eggs. knead until fully combined and the bottom of the bowl is clean (1-2 minutes).
3. wrap the dough in plastic and refrigerate 3-4 hours.
4. Remove dough and roll out to about ¼" thick. Press firmly into a greased pie tin.
5. Bake at 320° F for 7-12 minutes or until golden brown. Let cool.
6. fill crust with crème pâtissière (from croquembouche recipe) — remember to whisk before using — about ¾ full. Top the tart with any sliced fruit or berries, and powdered sugar.

No. 9
Our Wall

Me & my friends

Young boys are territorial. It is an instinctual thing, I think—a sort of rite of passage on the journey to becoming men. My friends and I were such boys. We laid particular claim to an outer wall of the first school that I attended. This was our territory and we defended it with the fiercest sort of pride.

We basically did so because the fattest *escargot* could be found on this wall, and catching them earned us a bit of money. After my one friend and I would pry the *escargot* from the wall, the other friend would clean them. How he came across such knowledge, we had no idea. But somehow, the boy knew to line cages with salt and herbs, place the *escargot* on these beds of seasoning, and patiently wait for a few days. Then he would rinse them. This method would rid the snails of any grit or impurities, and once they were cooked in fragrant garlic and creamy butter, the *escargot* would become flavorful supplication for the discerning palates of the patrons of the local restaurant.

While we waited on the escargot to be thoroughly and properly cleaned, we would make our way to the Loire River to catch our fair share of *gougeon*. These tiny fish were prized in our region, and it was no small feat to catch

35

them. My friends and I would stand on the riverbanks and stomp our feet to disrupt the water. Doing so sent the fish darting in a panic, and we would swoop in with our nets to catch as many as possible.

These plump snails and little fish would magically turn into meager treasure to line our small pockets after we sold them to the nearby restaurant. The *escargot* were purchased by the dozen, and we loved having as many of them as possible in our possession, because they brought more money than the fish did. The old man that ran the restaurant would count both the fish and the *escargot* with a sharp eye. He was not overly generous. We only earned a few coins for our effort, and by the time we divided these amongst the three of us, it was a mere pittance. Even so, as the coins rubbed together and jingled in our pockets, we felt as rich as kings.

ESCARGOT PROVENÇAL

serves 4

ingredients:

1/4 cup olive oil
1 ea. red onion, julienne
4 cloves garlic, minced
3 ea. anchovy filet
1 cup white wine
1 ea. small eggplant, peeled, small diced
1 ea. red bell pepper, roasted, julienne
1/2 cup kalamata olive, chopped

2 tsp. Herbs de Provence, dried
1 ea. bay leaf
1 tomato, diced
1/2 bunch parsley, chopped
salt & pepper
24 ea. escargots, large, preferably from France

directions:

1. Preheat the oven to 350° F.
2. Heat the oil in a small saucepan and sweat the onions, garlic, and anchovy, until the onions are translucent.
3. Raise the heat and deglaze with the white wine. Reduce by 1/4.
4. Add the eggplant, bell pepper, olives, dried herbs, bay leaf, and tomato.
5. Lower the heat and simmer for 20-25 minutes, covered, stirring occasionally.
6. Add the parsley and season to taste with salt and pepper.
7. If the mixture becomes too dry, add a little chicken broth or water.
8. Rinse the escargots and place them in a small baking dish or oven-proof sauté pan. Cover with the sauce and bake at 350° F for 20-25 minutes.
9. Let sit 5 minutes before serving with your favorite toasted bread.

No. 10
Fishing with the Resistance

I learned how to fish from a spy. It wasn't as exciting as a scene straight from the likes of a James Bond movie, but it is true all the same. A gentleman, Père Riou, resided in our village. He was in his late sixties to early seventies and rode around the village on his bicycle. I always found it entertaining that he kept all of his fishing lures and equipment tied to his bike. Père Riou captivated me because of the stories that wound themselves around him like the scarf that he wore about his neck.

Père Riou was extremely well known in our village because he worked for the largest train station in our area, the Gare de Saint Pierre des Corp. What especially mesmerized us all was the fact that he was also a member of The Resistance—a group of French citizens who adamantly opposed witnessing any part of France falling into the hands of the Germans. Père Riou was an integral player in many missions as a younger man, and more importantly, the Germans never once caught him. After the war passed, he had aged considerably, and his work was completed, Père Riou settled down. But the twinkle never left his eye and the spirit of what The Resistance had meant to him quite obviously never left his soul.

Imagine this interesting man and a young boy such as myself becoming friends. *Incroyable, oui, mais vrai*—incredible, yes, but true. Père Riou would come by the bakery to inquire about me, and we would spend much of my available free time down by the river. He taught me to fish for both *sandre poisson*—what you would call walleye—and for *brochet*—what you would know as pike.

Walleye fishing was relatively simple. When the Loire River's level was down, there would be pockets of sand that encased deeper water. The walleye could be found here, and they were plentiful. Pike fishing was much more difficult, but they were a joy to catch, as they made for a delicious feast.

My mother could not cook *brochet au beurre blanc*. Ahh, but my aunt could. Imagine the wafting aroma from mild, tender, flaky fish—caught by my own hands, no less— and resting in a delectable creamy sauce made from butter, shallots, and a little fresh lemon juice for brightness. I tell you—it was simply sublime, so much so that the dish is still popular in France. I completely understand why.

brochet au beurre blanc

Ingredients:

4 Pike Filet / 4 Walleye Filet   1 onion, studded with 6 cloves
1 qt. water   1 branch thyme
1 cup dry white wine   2 bay leaves
2 cloves garlic, mashed   salt & pepper

Combine all, and simmer for 20 minutes on the stove. Place
fish in the broth and cook 6-10 minutes, depending on the size.

Sauce ingredients:

2 shallots, diced very thin   1/4 cup white wine vinegar
10 oz. butter   1/4 cup white wine

In a small sauce pot, combine white wine, vinegar, and
shallots. Sweat until all liquid is gone. Gradually add the
butter by the tablespoon and whip it with the shallots. The
consistency should become a fluffy sauce.
Pour sauce over fish and serve with oven-roasted potatoes.

No. 11
Yellow Buses and Red Cherries

Me on my bike

Around the age of twelve, life began to take quite the turn for my family. Because of the army contract my father made with our friend, Guillaume, our bakery's small size was no longer serving my parents' needs. My father wanted to expand in our village, however this was not possible. Instead, he found what he was searching for in another town—the opportunity to purchase not one, but three bakeries! He jumped at the chance.

Our current village was a lower income sort of area, which meant that the people spent their money more so on bread and less on meat. Bread was much less expensive. It nourished families and spread their food budgets much farther. My father knew, in our move away from his original bakery that burnt, that a smaller bakery would be successful in such a town, and he made a decent wage for our family, accordingly. In his original planning, though, he did not take into account a potential army contract.

The new town that my father found was a much higher income neighborhood, so the opposite here was true. The townspeople spent more of their wages on meat and used bread as an accompaniment to their meals. When my father realized that this town held the potential for three bakeries, he wanted to own them all. He planned to turn one into a production center, and sell what he fashioned both there, as well as in the other two stores. These would be used purely for selling bread, and not for production. In such a town, more store locations with no immediate competition—on top of the army's business—would ensure that we would thrive. I believe that I mentioned previously that my father was quite the businessman!

It was not an easy transition. My father wanted everything to be seamless, so he and my mother worked very hard to keep our current bakery running—to provide for the family—as well as to get the new bakeries operational, simultaneously. It took almost two years to set up the new bakeries for production, and to sell the old one. The process demanded much. The hours were long and the loans were big, but the promise of the success from the move was even bigger. That kept us all going.

About a year into the transition, in July, we moved to an apartment across the street from the new production bakery. My life would change dramatically because of this move. We were now living in a bigger area, and as my parents were so busy with bakery details, I was enrolled in school to keep me occupied. I would take the bus to school every day through the week, and I would pretty much only work at our still-functioning bakery on Sundays. That bakery was now located twenty kilometers away from where we were currently living.

To get to our old village, I relied on my bicycle and the energy of my own two legs! Riding in the early morning from apartment to bakery, and then again later that evening from bakery to apartment, was arduous. Thankfully, in-between, there was a grand old cherry tree on the edge of the roadway. Its thick, brown trunk provided support for my weary back to lean against, and its dense foliage suspended shade over my sweaty brow.

And the cherries—the tree was overloaded with them! The cherries burst with sweetness in my mouth, and on those hot days were the perfect refreshment. I would often be rather gluttonous. My fingers and tongue were constantly stained from their bounty. But I would always

42

pick extra to take to my mother. She could make a *clafoutis* with cherries that was simply divine.

The dough was sweet and rustic and studded with the cherries that I had picked. It would puff up in the oven before collapsing and the center had a soft, almost custard-like, quality while the edges were browned and crisp. I would devour her creation just as wolfishly as I did nature's roadside offering.

Clafoutis aux Cerises

ingredients for 4 servings:

1 lb. fresh cherries
2 big eggs
4 to 5 oz. powdered sugar
2 oz. cake flour
8 oz. milk
Vanilla extract
½ oz. butter

directions:

1. Wash, dry the cherries, and take out their stems.
2. For the little cherries, remove their pits.
3. Preheat the oven to 375° F.
4. Whip the eggs, add the sugar, and, little by little, add the cake flour.
5. Whip everything again and add the milk and the vanilla.
6. Butter the clafoutis mold.
7. Layer the cherries in the mold, and pour the batter on top.
8. Put into the oven and bake for 40-45 minutes.
   To verify your clafoutis is baked, stick a knife into it and it should come out dry.
9. Sprinkle the clafoutis with powder sugar.

No. 12
Apprenticeship with Damien

As I previously mentioned, life in this new town changed considerably for all of us. My father was now the leader of three bakeries. His production center employed two full-time pastry chefs, three bakers plus himself, and all three bakeries utilized front of the house staff. On average, three to four thousand baguettes were produced, as well as a mountainous amount of croissants and the petit pans that the army still required. Many new and exciting treats were now offered, as well, thanks to my father's pastry chefs. It was a full-scale operation.

My mother no longer had to make delivery runs as she once had. She was now the overseer for the main bakery. She even stopped pastry making completely—except to provide our family with enjoyment. She now worked the front of the house only. My sister continued with her education and her love of culture. I did not spend much time with her, as our lives were both spinning in much different circles.

I was around fourteen years old at this time. I worked at the bakery, attended school, began taking Judo lessons in my limited amount of free time, and hung out with my new friend, Bastien. Because this village was so much larger than the old one and was a much higher income neighborhood, more opportunities were available for the village youth.

I found a new wall, but I did not claim it as my own, like in my previous village. This wall was close to the church and a hangout spot for all of the local teenagers. Bastien and I socialized here since all of the village girls did, too. We were typical teenage boys for certain. I saved the spare money that my father grudgingly shoved my way for all of my hard work at the bakery and bought my first true prize with it—a Malaguti. This motorcycle was a stylish replacement for my worn out bicycle.

Life carried on this way for me until the age of sixteen. Then, my father decided that traditional school was no longer a necessity. He insisted that I would apprentice and become a baker. I had absolutely no desire to do so, as I was not interested in bread, or turning into my father. I agreed, with one condition. I would quit school, and I would apprentice at the bakery, but only with one of his pastry chefs.

There were always three apprentices in the bakery at any given time—a first year, a second year, and a third year apprentice. This was the hierarchy of the training that was given. Since I already knew so much about pastries, from working so closely with my mother, I was automatically enlisted as a second year apprentice. I was proud of my accomplishments. And the fact that I no longer had to work with bread in any capacity was a cause for celebration!

Damien was a new, young pastry chef in my father's employ. In fact, he was only about four years older than me. What he lacked in age, he more than made up for in ability. I learned so much from him.

Baking Away

His skillset was on a completely different level than what I was accustomed to. Damien was a very talented pastry chef, and he became a very good friend to me.

We created delicacies both sweet and savory and sold many of these to the village lunch crowd, much like I now do at Our Daily Bread. Such specialties were in high demand. This was all very new to me then, as I was only accustomed to selling bread and a limited variety of pastries.

A house favorite was Vol-au-vent. This was basically the French-style of chicken potpie. Light and flaky puff pastry dough was stuffed with roasted chicken, mushrooms, onions, garlic, and seasonings. These ingredients were cradled in a delicate, creamy white sauce and then baked until piping hot. These flew off of our shelves, and understandably so. My mouth still waters when I think about them.

Vol au Vent

ingredients:
1 patty shell (from your favorite bakery)
1 lbs. white sauce ←
1 lbs. chanterelle mushrooms
1 large carrot
½ onion
1 clove garlic
½ cup white wine
4 chicken breasts, cooked and diced
cream, as needed
1 tbsp. butter

1 lbs. butter
1 lbs. flour
1 gallon milk
1 qt. cream
salt, pepper, nutmeg

directions:
1. Sautee mushrooms, carrots, onion, garlic, and butter. Add the chicken breast and white wine.
2. Add 1 lbs. white sauce, then add the cream to make sauce more liquidy.
3. Pour into patty shell.

Mice and Men

B eing an apprentice was not an easy task. Every Tuesday through Sunday, I had to wake at three a.m. to clock in at work by three-thirty. Thankfully, on Mondays we were given a break. I spent most of my time working and had very little opportunity for extracurricular activities. My socializing was limited to Saturday nights when I could meet with friends and attend the movies.

My friend Damien

Damien made sure that I could at least take part in that much, and for that, I was grateful.

But, being a typical teenage boy, I constantly pushed the boundaries. I would stay out as late as I could on Saturday nights, and I would oversleep and make it to work late on Sundays without fail. Unfortunately, this did not go unnoticed by my father, and I paid the price for my tardiness. Nonetheless, the following week, I would do the same thing all over again. I was a bit stubborn, needless to say.

Pastry production for the bakery was located in the basement, but dry storage and our refrigeration was located in a room on an upper level. One Sunday morning—late as usual—Damien sent me upstairs to bring down a case of eggs. This was my punishment for my lateness. These were not ordinary cartons like you would purchase at your grocery store. Each case held 360 eggs. The containers were huge! So much so, that they made quite the bed for an overly tired young boy to lie upon. Two hours later, Damien found me curled up asleep on top of those egg cartons. What can I say? I was exhausted and it was much too tempting!

Thankfully, Damien wasn't too tough on me because of it. He was much more easy-going than my father. Due to this nature, he fell victim to many, many pranks. The apprentices *loved* to play pranks on him. I still laugh every time that I recall the look on his face when he opened up the box of matches to light the stove one morning only to find a live mouse in the matchbox. We laughed for days! Damien hated mice. Truly hated them. After the initial shock, he took the prank in stride—just as he did with all of the others that we played upon him.

Do not be deceived—our days were not always filled with fun and games. Of course, every chance that could be found, we worked in small ways to entertain ourselves. However, we labored tirelessly and for long hours to produce the pastries that my father's three bakeries required.

After my day's labor was completed, I would be ravenously hungry. One of the ladies in our village owned and operated a *crepe* shop across from the bus station where I used to catch the bus that would take me to school. Her *crepes* were delicious, and whenever I could scrape together some spare change, I would stop by her shop.

It was a tiny establishment, and the scent of *crepes* tickled my nose and my taste buds as soon as I walked in the door. My favorite selection was the savory stuffed buckwheat *crepe*. The tartness of the buckwheat in the crisp *crepe* complemented the creaminess of the eggs and cheese and the saltiness of the ham that was generously stuffed inside. Even though I was learning every day from Damien's instruction, and I was more than impressed with his creations, I looked forward to frequenting the kind village woman's shop and sampling this delicate concoction.

Buckwheat Crepes Stuffed with eggs, cheese, & ham

CREPES

ingredients:

1 cup wheat flour

¼ cup white flour

2 ¼ tsp. salt

3 cups milk

4 large eggs

4 oz butter, melted

Directions:

combine all ingredients in a large bowl, using a whisk. using a half cup, pour the batter onto a sprayed pan or flat griddle. cook for 30-45 seconds then set aside.

filling

ingredients:

2 slices ham

2 eggs

2 slices swiss cheese

Directions:

cook both slices of ham and both eggs in the style of your choice. Lay a slice of swiss cheese on top of 2 separate crepes. place the ham and eggs on one of the crepes, then flip the other one on top (so the cheese is on the inside). sprinkle with parsley and shredded cheese if desired.

No. 14
Soap Bubbles and Steve McQueen

I've mentioned before that even though my life was fully consumed with work during the years of my apprenticeship, Damien and I always found ways to inject a bit of fun into our days. Such is an inherent quality of being young, I suppose. We were typical boys. We chased girls, loved our motorcycles, and we were town pranksters.

I will never forget how one midnight, after a night of socializing, we sneaked toward the fountain in the town square armed with a bottle of soap. The next day, the local newspaper reported about the inexplicable mountain of bubbles that poured from the fountain. We kept our cool and only laughed hysterically at our tomfoolery out of earshot of anyone else, of course. Somehow, we were never caught, and to this day, we have yet to be!

What bonded Damien and me even more than our love of pranks was our love of motorcycles. I still owned my Malaguti, but I didn't fully come to an appreciation of motorcycles until Damien showed me the way. He was crazy for them. So crazy, in fact, that for the two years I apprenticed with him, and no matter how busy we were, we always found the opportunity to attend the races in Le Mans.

Le Mans was located approximately eighty kilometers away from our village. There were two major races held there every year, a motorcycle race known as the Bol d'Or, as well as an automobile race—the Vingt-Quatre Le Mans. Both of these races, as it suggests in the name of the car race, were twenty-four hours long, and both were wildly popular. Steve McQueen added to the fame and popularity of the auto race with the release of his 1971 movie, *Le Mans*. The movie contains actual footage from the 1970 race.

Damien and I would spend race days with our eyes practically popping out of our heads from visions of those cars, and later on in the year, from our favorites—the motorcycles. We were like two children in a candy store— except that the treats weren't composed of sugar, but of metal and rubber. And the food that we would bring with us on these journeys—it was a tailgater's fantasy.

We always brought *mergez*, an African style sausage perfumed with the spices of lands foreign to us, and housed in familiar baguettes or croissants. But my favorite by far was the *rillets.* This was a Loire Valley specialty sandwich. Delectable pork belly, salty and ribboned with fat, was cut into squares and then boiled on the stovetop. It could be served warm right off the stove, but Damien and I put it into a cooler for our journey. This was fine by me, because I always preferred it cold. We ate it with mustard and cornichons on baguettes. *C'est magnifique!* In fact, I don't know which was more enjoyable for me—the races or the food!

I do know one thing for sure—these races meant more to us than just flashy automobiles and motorcycles paired with delicious food for our consumption. They meant freedom. We weren't merely a pastry chef and his apprentice on those days. We were two friends—two men— experiencing the richness that life offered, and tasting a glimpse of what lay beyond our everyday existence.

rillettes

ingredients:

5 lbs. PORK butt, 1" dice
8 ea. bay leaves
½ cup cognac
2 cups chicken stock
salt and pepper, to taste

directions:

1. Preheat oven to 300° F.
2. Using a sauce pan that is just large enough to hold the pork, heat over medium heat until hot.
3. Add the pork and bay leaves.
4. Stirring frequently, cook the pork until it has released a good amount of liquid.
5. Turn the heat to high and add the cognac and chicken stock. Season with salt and pepper.
6. Once boiling, lower the heat and cook at a slight simmer, covered, for 1 hour. Stir occasionally.
7. After 1 hour check for tenderness. The pork should pull apart very easily with two forks. If there is any resistance, replace the lid and cook another 15 minutes, continuously checking until tender.
8. Remove from stove and let cool until you are able to handle it. Using either your hands or a mixer, shred the meat finely. Don't over mix so as not to turn it into a paste.
9. Place in glass containers and store in the fridge. Enjoy on toast with cornichon and whole grain mustard.

No. 15
Les Compagnons du Devoir

After two long years, at the ripe, old age of eighteen, my training with Damien came to an end. I graduated from my apprenticeship at the top of my class, which was quite an honor. Apprenticeship came naturally to me. I was the fastest in my class when it came to prep work, and because I was born into work such as this, I knew the job well even before I began my training.

I could have chosen to stay at my father's bakery. It certainly would have been a logical choice, but I was ready to spread my wings and further my training at the same time. So, when I was accepted to the prestigious school, Les Compagnons du Devoir, I was beyond ecstatic. It was exactly what I had wished for.

The name Les Compagnons du Devoir, when translated, means "the companions of duty, or devotion." It was and still is an institution devoted to training young professionals to both live and work properly. This school was special because it recognized and championed the need to send prepared, productive members of society out into the world. Our instructors not only trained us in areas of potential employment, but they also taught us how to live. Here, I learned to respect myself, others, and life itself. I learned how to grow to become a good, responsible man.

Mostly every large town in France contained a branch of the school. While I studied, there were around thirty to forty schools in existence, spread all across only France. Tours, in the area in which I was from, was one of the top Compagnonique towns in France. However I attended school in the town of Nîmes, which was—geographically speaking—close to Avignon and roughly 1,200 kilometers from my hometown

The schools trained not just bakers and pastry chefs, but also carpenters, stonemasons, plumbers, roofers—most any job that required a person to work with their hands. In fact, the very crafters of your own Statue of Liberty received their training from Les Compagnons du Devoir. Schooling was only available to men at that time, and only French men, at that. We slept, ate, and learned all in the same building. Each department had its own classrooms, but we were not only taught information and skills that related to our potential trades. We were also taught traditional subjects, such as math and grammar.

We had separate bedrooms and a dining hall in the dormitory section of the building. Only men were allowed around the sleeping quarters—no female visitors or relatives—however we had house mothers that came in periodically to offer assistance and to attend to our needs. And every day, when we arrived to dinner, it was school policy that we dress formally in a tie and vest.

I learned how to make everything here: ice cream, chocolate, confections, and all aspects of pastry. Though the training from my apprenticeship was a large step up from what I already knew, this was like a whole new world to me. One of the best things that I was taught was how to make buttercream. At the time, buttercream was not a trend, as it is today. It was a brand new concept created by Monsieur le Notre, a mentor and head pastry chef in Paris.

We fashioned a simple yellow cake and frosted it with decadent, fresh buttercream both inside and out. The buttercream was definitely the star of the show. Its sweet creaminess danced from my finger onto my tongue. Though it seemed to be an understated dessert, it was quite an elegant one—*très chic*—and its popularity has transcended decades. Understandably so—it is that delicious. I still serve a moist yellow cake with fresh strawberries today at Our Daily Bread. But since buttercream has become such a trend, I cover my cake with light, sinful, homemade whipped cream. The whipped cream adds a slight twist to the original concept, but the dessert is still crafted from the very training that I received so many years ago.

Yellow cake with whipped cream icing & fresh strawberries

Ingredients:

.75 oz. butter
2 lbs. sugar
1½ tbsp. vanilla
6 eggs
.6 lbs. all-purpose flour

1 lbs. cake flour
1½ tsp. baking soda
.5 tbs. salt
3 cups buttermilk
fresh strawberries, as needed
whipped cream (for icing)

Directions:

1. Cream the butter, sugar, and vanilla until it reaches a light, fluffy texture.
2. Add the eggs, 2 or 3 at a time, until combined.
3. In a separate bowl, mix together the flour, cake flour, baking soda, and salt. Gradually add them into the batter, stirring continuously.
4. Add the buttermilk. Scrape the bowl with the spatula and make sure the batter is smooth.
5. Bake in a cake pan
6. Once cake has cooled, cut it in half to create 2 layers. Brush the inside of both layers with a kirsch simple syrup.
   → KIRSCH SIMPLE SYRUP: 5 oz. water + 2.5 oz. sugar + 2 oz. kirsch
   (combine and boil — as soon as it begins to boil, remove from heat.)
7. On one half of the cake, spread the whipped cream and fill with sliced strawberries. Reassemble the cake and frost the entire outside with whipped cream. Top with halved strawberries.

No. 16
Lost Recipes

During our attendance at Les Compagnons du Devoir, part-time employment in our particular area of training was also arranged for us. Most of our salaries went to the school to cover the cost of boarding, while we were allowed to keep a small portion. I was placed with Monsieur Liton. He was a robust man in his mid-forties, and the bakery that he had acquired had been in existence for one hundred years. However, it was a recent purchase of his, so he was in desperate need of assistance.

I was the Monsieur's very first apprentice, and neither of us knew quite what to expect. He knew nothing of my skills or capabilities. As I had only worked for my father in some form or another, this was all quite new to me, as well. Even so, our relationship thrived. So much so, that in the twenty-two years that he ran that particular bakery, he continually employed apprentices from Les Compagnons.

The Monsieur was a knowledgeable man and a good teacher. I learned much from him in the time that we spent together. He was especially well known in chocolates and only worked with the best chocolate that our country offered. For us, this chocolate came from the chocolate-makers of Valrhona, which was located approximately one hundred kilometers from Monsieur Liton's bakery. We would buy large blocks of chocolate directly from them on a consistent basis. I had never tasted chocolate of such fine quality before! Rich dark silk flirted with my taste buds.

Palets d'Or

The Monsieur created divine samplings with this chocolate. One in particular was well known in France: Palet d'Or. This confection was formed from a special chocolate recipe and decorated with a small design fashioned from gold leaf. Multiple times, I asked the Monsieur to share the recipe with me, or at least allow me the opportunity to assist in creating the delicacy. Excuses were all that he offered. "You already have enough to work on," or "Don't you remember? I already gave you that recipe. You must have lost it!"

This happened over and over, until it actually became rather comical—like a game to me. For the year and a half that I worked alongside him, I was never given the recipe. I did not mind.

Forty years later, my wife and I visited the Monsieur. He was still spry, even for being in his eighties, and no longer in the chocolate-making business. I thought that my chance at finally being given the recipe had arrived! I asked him once more for the recipe, and his eyes twinkled as he replied, "I don't know how you keep losing this recipe! I will give it to you one more time..." As our visit drew to a close, we spoke our goodbyes, and left him. He never gave me the recipe.

I still think of the old man with fondness. Even though that special, elusive recipe never became one that I could call my own, the knowledge and skill that I took away from my time with him is invaluable. And, trust me, I came away with plenty of other recipes for delectable confections. One in particular—a Grand Marnier chocolate truffle—takes me back to that time in my life every time that I taste its dark decadence. And, as you can see, I haven't forgotten to share the recipe with you.

truffles

Ingredients:

1/4 lbs. dark chocolate   Sifted cocoa powder, as needed
1/4 lbs. milk chocolate
1/4 lbs. heavy cream
.15 lbs. Grand Marnier

Directions:

1. Boil the heavy cream and pour it on top of the dark chocolate. Add the Grand Marnier and mix until smooth. Refrigerate overnight.
2. Remove from fridge and shape into marble-sized balls. Refrigerate again until needed.
3. Melt the dark chocolate in the microwave at 30-second intervals, stirring in between. Prepare a separate small container of the cocoa powder and set it next to the melted chocolate.
4. Remove the balls from the fridge — they should be fairly hard. One by one, drop each ball in the chocolate, coating it entirely. Use a fork to pick it up and shake off excess chocolate. Then drop it in the cocoa powder, rolling it around until completely hard. Pick it up with a sifter to allow excess cocoa powder to fall off. Repeat until all garnish is used.

No. 17
La Feria

Nîmes was not just known as the town that housed Les Compagnons du Devoir. The town's history was quite evident, even to the inexperienced onlooker. Nîmes was a very Romanesque town. The largest aqueduct in France could be found there, as well as one of the most beautiful arenas located in the south of France. Once upon a time, traditional Roman games used to be held in that very arena. Even the townspeople spoke a different, heavier dialect of French than I was accustomed to. It was all very interesting, *certainement*.

There was also a Spanish influence in Nîmes, and this was never more evident than during La Feria. La Feria is a huge festival that is held in the arena and the streets surrounding it. This festival actually takes place on a Friday-Saturday-Sunday twice a year—both in the spring, at Whitsun, and in the fall, at harvest time. During La Feria, the town is alive with horses and bulls, games and competitions, live music, dancing in the street, food, wine, and revelry.

In my day, as well as today, in keeping with Spanish heritage, there was a running of the bulls in the streets. There were all sorts of other bull related activities throughout the town, including bullfights and games in the arena. My favorite game to watch pitted sleek men against the bulls in a game of catch the ring. Each bull would have a blue ring secured to his forehead right between the horns, and the game player would attempt to grab the ring with a handheld hook. This was a game of bravery and skill, and only attempted by professionals, or the ultra daring.

For fun, and a bit of comic relief for the crowd, a similar game was arranged for the youth of the town. Instead of bulls, the rings were secured to slightly wild and crazy cows! But the young competitors took the game just as seriously as the adults did. Retrieving the ring awarded the winner bragging rights for the duration of the festival.

French influence could be found in the street food that was sold during La Feria. An especially delicious offering was a specialty of the town—Les Pâté de Nîmes. Flaky *quiche* dough was formed into a hollow ball, and then allowed to dry for roughly a day. After dried, the dough was stuffed with a hearty mixture of seasoned pork and veal, onions, garlic, and herbs. The opening was then topped with another piece of delicate dough, baked, and served either warm or cold on the street. It was a festival—one for the senses!

Everyone could experience whichever sort of fun was most longed for at La Feria, and some took a little too much advantage of this! The authorities formed a creative—and ultimately humorous—way to handle the revelers. If someone were too drunk or disorderly, and acting accordingly, the police would simply tie that person up to the trunk of a nearby tree! About an hour, accompanied by much laughter and finger pointing from passersby, was usually all it took for that person to agree to amend his ways. The authorities would then loosen the person with no other caution than to party a little more responsibly or suffer a similar fate once more. Ahh, some revelers needed an extra hour or two, and yes, sometimes even multiple times of restraining to calm their shenanigans.

I will leave it to your imagination if I made an intimate acquaintance with a tree trunk or two during my La Feria experience, or not. But I will say this: for a teenage boy such as me, La Feria was much more than a mere festival. It was an adventure, and one that I will never forget.

les pate des Nimes

dough
ingredients:
8 oz. FLOUR   water, as needed
4 oz. soft butter   pinch of black pepper

Combine all ingredients with hands to form a dough.

filling
ingredients:
4 oz. ground pork   1 egg
4 oz. ground veal   1 shallot, diced
1 oz. cognac   1 clove garlic, thinly diced
salt & pepper

Directions:
1. Roll out dough on flat surface to about 1/8" thick. Use a circular cutter to punch out a piece of dough that will line a muffin tin. Press the dough into the tin to make a cup.
2. Combine all of the filling ingredients, and fill the dough cup. use the remaining dough to create a "lid".
3. Bake for about 25 minutes at 360-370 °F. Remove from pan and serve with green salad.

Frustrations

Life has a way of turning on its head in the passing of a moment, doesn't it? I had attended Les Compagnons du Devoir for around a year and a half, and I enjoyed the direction in which I was headed. Things were moving along at a smooth, even pace, until a surprise roadblock sent my journey down a different, yet familiar, path. I suddenly became desperately ill and had no choice but to leave school. With nowhere else to go except home, I returned—but certainly with little enthusiasm.

My teenage years

Even as unhappy as I was to be there, I decided to give working with my father another attempt. I chose to work alongside him once more in the production of bread, because I wanted to further my skillset. I had worked rather extensively with pastries up to that point. For a while, all was well. A couple of months in, I came to recognize that this decision seemed to have been a mistake. As before, our personalities clashed, and even more frustrations began to rise within me.

These frustrations turned themselves into errant, rebellious, youthful behaviors. I was heading down a slightly questionable path, *certainement*. And, as it often happens, when life is dark, we must move forward through even more darkness before we make our way into the light. For me, this darkness took the form of a random kitchen accident.

Very early one morning, I was at work in the bakery, and not quite awake. (As you will recall, a baker's workday begins well before sunrise.) A commercial machine was mixing that morning's dough, as always. Our production was on such a large scale that we did not mix the dough by hand.

Somehow the dough found its way into the motor of the mixing machine. Even though there were tools to retrieve the dough, and even though I knew better, I reached in to loosen the dough. It was a mistake I have regretted ever since. That misstep cost me the top of my left index finger.

I was out of work for a month due to my accident. I never wanted to touch bread again. Eventually I changed my mind, yet for the moment, I was both irritated and defeated. I was frustrated with bread. I was frustrated with pastries and the fact that I could not continue my training. I was frustrated with my father. I was frustrated with life. It was a very dark time for me.

With time, I healed both physically and mentally. When I was ready to go back to work, I could not continue with my training at Les Compagnons, and I did not wish to continue on at my father's bakery. So I searched for new opportunities, and finally some light appeared. A *mademoiselle* in our town needed assistance as she had taken over her father's catering business after his sudden passing. In those days, men normally ran businesses, so such an arrangement was quite *nouveau*. But I did not care about the unconventionality—I needed work!

I already possessed limited experience with catering. My father's production bakery was very large, and in the midst of my apprenticeship with Damien, my father took a part of this store and dedicated it to catering. He hired a chef, and I learned the ins and outs of catering from him. Slowly, I was learning about the art of food. It was just the beginning.

As I worked with the *mademoiselle,* I learned even more. She gave me a deeper glimpse into the business side of catering. Such knowledge would prove quite useful to me in later years when I was ready to open businesses of my own. To this day, I am still very appreciative of the information that I acquired.

It was her skill with food that I valued the most. My love of the intricacies and the nuances of food grew every day that I worked alongside this woman. She showcased delicious combinations in her *canapé* and *charcuterie*. And her Salmon Chaud Froid was beautiful.

Translated into English, *chaud froid* literally means hot/cold. The salmon was hot in the beginning, when cooked, then placed in the cooler to chill. The skin was then taken off the fish, it was glazed with a glossy gelatin, and then served cold with decorative vegetable *crudités*. A mayonnaise-based tartar style sauce was served on the side for dipping. It was a favorite of her customers, and I still offer it today through my catering at Our Daily Bread.

At home, I serve a similar, simpler version of this dish, however. Rather than deal with the prep work and the glossing of the fish, I prepare salmon with a leek cream sauce for my family. The luscious cream and the snap of the leeks, much like a necklace that drips of diamonds graces the throat of a beautiful woman, accent the fresh, wild cut of tender salmon. It is truly a delicious dish.

Yes, with this new catering position, I was able to begin my journey from my previous darkness toward the light. I did not realize it then, but my life would soon change in a huge way. This new direction in my pilgrimage would ultimately lead me to the true light of my life—an introduction to the woman who would become my wife.

Salmon with leek cream sauce

Ingredients:

6 oz salmon, 4 ea.	1/4 cup parmesan cheese
1 leek, small diced	salt & pepper, to taste
1 onion, small diced	1/4 tsp. nutmeg
4 cloves garlic, minced	1 tbsp. parsley, chopped
2 cups heavy cream	
4 oz white wine	

Directions:

1. Preheat oven to 350° F. Heat 2 tbsp. olive oil in a sautee pan. Sear the salmon on high heat for 5 minutes on each side, then put it in a small baking dish. Cook in oven for 10 minutes.
2. While salmon is cooking, sweat the onions, leeks, and garlic until the onions are translucent. Turn to high heat and deglaze with white wine. Reduce by half.
3. Add heavy cream. Simmer until reduced by half.
4. Add the parmesan and nutmeg, then season with salt and pepper. Add the parsley.
5. Serve salmon with sauce on the side.

No. 19
Drafted!

Me in army

In the midst of my catering work, my life's journey would take another very different turn. In late May of 1977, I received a notice that I had been drafted into the army. At this time, the French government drafted typically every male between the ages of nineteen and twenty-one for one year of service. The government quit drafting citizens in the mid-eighties, but since I was twenty years old in 1977, I fit the bill. There was nothing that I could do about it, and heeding the government's call, on June 1st I reported for duty in the army.

I served in the town of Compiègne. The area held distinct historical significance. Here, the Armistice with Germany agreed to end WWI in November of 1918. This took place in a railroad carriage in nearby Le Francport. It made me proud to know that I was serving my country in an area that had once been of such great importance.

We knew the six-week-long period of basic training— what Americans call boot camp—as, "The Class." Here, we were trained in guns and learned about fighting. It was very structured and physical. I was fine with the physical aspect, because years of practicing Judo had left me in top shape. The structure took a bit of getting used to. My life had been structured during my time at Les Compagnons du Devoir, or in my various jobs, but nothing like this! It was exactly what I needed. It moved me away from those rebellious, youthful behaviors that I previously mentioned and sent me down a more proper path.

Because I was so physically fit, I graduated in third place from my class. As a reward for finishing so close to the top of my class, I was allowed to choose which duty I wanted to perform to complete the remainder of my service. I chose to serve as a pastry chef in the restaurant that provided food for the officers. Understand that only the officers—and on Sunday's, their families—were allowed to eat at this particular restaurant.

This was a very special position. I had chosen well for myself, and I ate very well, accordingly. The regular servicemen did not eat nearly as generously as we who worked in the officer's restaurant, because they were limited in their rations and in the quality of food that was served. Since I worked for the higher-ranking officials, there were no budget restrictions or rations and the positive effects of this trickled down to servicemen such as myself.

I had never worked in a kitchen like this before— twenty-two men performed tasks here! There were butchers, bartenders, and men devoted to creating sauces— just to name a few. Every department, except for pastry, employed two to three men. I, however, was the only one that worked in my department. Even though we were young, we were all excellent at the labor that we performed. Only the best of the best were chosen to take care of the officer's restaurant.

It was a beautiful environment in which to learn. Here, the fire of cooking fine food that had kindled under the supervision of my previous catering position truly fanned into a flame. I learned so much: how to tend bar, how to clean and butcher whole animals into gorgeous cuts of meat, how to create tasteful renditions of the mother sauces—basically, I learned how to understand food.

We served breakfast, lunch, and dinner, and we used only the top of the line ingredients. For instance, we would take a van every week to the province of Champagne just to purchase the sweet, bubbly beverage that supplied the restaurant. Everything that came from our kitchen was made from scratch. Since we didn't have to deal with profits or accountability, we could do or create whatever we wanted or whatever was asked of us. Needless to say, creativity flowed.

Such creativity was displayed on the plate every single day. A memorable example of this dealt with a very popular fish of the time—the *barbu**. We marinated this fish overnight in a top burgundy wine, Chambertin*. This was quite the unconventional method, as fish isn't typically cooked in red wine, except the earthy characteristics of this particular wine, along with its crisp acidity, made it the perfect choice. The wine was further reduced with flavorful shallots to create a lovely sauce to serve atop the mild, delicate fish. The sauce flowed across the tongue like satin. The dish was an experiment in creative cooking that dazzled the palates of our patrons.

Recipe Notes: While *barbu* is still available for purchase today, it is not as common in inland areas. Fresh grouper can provide an ample substitution. And, if Chambertin cannot be found, a savory Pinot Noir will work well, as that grape provides the base and flavor profile for the Chambertin.

grouper in Chambertin Sauce

ingredients:

4 oz. shallots	1 bottle Chambertin Red wine
4 tbsp. butter	4 filet of grouper (6-7 oz. pieces)
1 clove garlic	Pinch of Old Bay seasoning
~~xxxxxxxxxxxx~~	Salt & Pepper
400 mL fish stock	

directions:

1. Marinate the grouper in Red wine for 2 hours. After 2 hours, remove the fish and save the wine as you will be using it for your sauce.
2. Sautee 2 tbsp. butter & the shallots until lightly brown. Add pepper and the garlic, cooking another 3-4 minutes.
3. Add the Red wine and the fish stock. Reduce to ⅓, and add the remaining 2 tbsp. butter.
4. In a separate pan, sautee the grouper with butter. Pour the sauce over the fish, and continue cooking until done. Enjoy with another bottle of Chambertin!

No. 20
Just Something About Jackets

It was true, the army structured my life, and I was a changed man. Ahh, but some things about me would not change, and this included my love of pranks. I suppose that the heart of a boy still beat within my chest. Damien was not there to join in the fun with me as he did when I lived at home, so I gravitated toward other friends with similar tastes.

One evening, our kitchen manager fell victim to our humor without even realizing it. The kitchen manager was not an officer, but he still held a much higher rank than my butcher friend, or me, so we were always supposed to show him respect. And we did respect him...nevertheless this regard did not make him immune to our pranks!

The manager wore a chef's jacket labeled with his name, as is still popular in most kitchens. He had a habit of leaving one extra jacket hanging in the office just in case something were to happen to the one that he was wearing. At the end of our shift, as we were finishing up our duties, that jacket hung in front of us, and we shared a devious glance. We "borrowed" the jacket and headed straight to town. We certainly showed off and raised quite the ruckus disguised the whole time as our superior. And we promptly returned our costume unscathed to its hanger in the office after our short bit of fun. Thankfully, no one was ever the wiser, as we could've been in huge trouble for such an escapade.

That jacket, and the name embroidered on it, stayed pristine. Unfortunately, one jacket I came into contact with did not, and there were no fun and games involved. As I previously mentioned to you, I learned much working in the officer's restaurant, and we were a fully staffed kitchen team. On occasion, there were gaps in certain positions, and we had to learn to step up to fill them. Accordingly, I was a waiter for one night—and one night only—after I accidentally dumped a whole tray of cocktails onto an officer's dress jacket! The management never asked me to wait tables again. From that night on, I mostly was tasked with what I knew best—pastry.

So I challenged myself at my position and constantly pushed my own boundaries and creative limits. I took pride, focused diligently on my pastry work, and devoted no time to boyish pranks while doing so. Many opportunities arose for me. Once, I baked a gigantic layer cake to serve three hundred people for a particular catered party. With my dedicated hands, I transformed the cake into an edible masterpiece.

I was shocked after it finally came together because I had never created anything of such beauty or stature. The cake towered above me and its luscious layers rose toward the ceiling. So much so that when it was time to move the cake from the kitchen to the dining room, I could not see where I was going. A rushing waiter focused on his duties opened the door into my cart and, the top of my cake fell to the floor! Catastrophe! I kept my cool, though, repaired the cake, and served it to the delight of the guests.

Another moment of pride arose when my Compiègne based team was personally requested to cater a communion party for the family of the French Air Force's top general.

In army with my grand creation

We rode to the general's home in the backs of luxurious cars. As I watched the French flags wave atop the hood of my transport, I realized just what an impressive invitation we had received. We showed off the best of our abilities that day and most certainly did not disappoint.

Even as superb as opportunities like these were, I felt the most pride and joy at the creativity that I was free to display in the restaurant. As I mentioned before, we had no monetary budget to stick to in our kitchen, so the best and freshest ingredients were always at our disposal. I took full advantage of this when I created my very first signature cake. I named this cake Noirmont because of its mountainous layers of dense, dark chocolate. These decadent layers were soaked in Cointreau-infused syrup, and the center of the cake held a surprise—a well of delicate Cointreau cream mousse. The exterior of the cake was covered in a rich, Cointreau ganache.

The bittersweet orange *apéritif* married beautifully with the bittersweet bite of the dark chocolate in a subtle harmony. The cake was so heavy and sinful that a small slice could satisfy even the sweetest tooth. It instantly became a restaurant favorite, especially with a particular official. Captain Gagnard and his family requested this cake practically every week. It became a Sunday tradition.

Ten years later, with my pranks and my army days well behind me, and my wife and children surrounding me, I operated a small bakery of my own in Martinique. I occasionally served Noirmont in my bakery. One random day, a certain lady patron asked her waitress, "Just who made this cake?" After the girl explained, she requested to meet me. Imagine the surprise on my face when none other than Madame Gagnard greeted me! Her husband had been stationed on the very island that my own family resided upon. *Il est un petite monde pour certains*—it is a small world for certain!

NOIRMONT CAKE

ingredients:
1 chocolate cake (either your own recipe or from a box)
creme patissiere (use recipe from croquembouche)
.5 lbs. whipping cream
~~1~~ cointreau
.5 lbs. dark chocolate
.5 lbs. heavy cream

directions:
1. whip .5 lbs. of creme patissiere with the whipping cream. Add 2 oz. of cointreau.
2. Cut the cake in half to create 2 layers. Brush both inner surfaces with a cointreau simple syrup.
   → COINTREAU SIMPLE SYRUP: 5 oz. water + 2.5 oz. sugar + 2 oz. cointreau (combine and boil—as soon as it starts to boil, remove from heat.)
3. Fill the cake with the cream from step 1. Re-assemble the layers and frost the outside as well.
4. Create your garnish. Boil the heavy cream and pour it on top of the dark chocolate to melt it. Leave for 5 minutes, then whisk until smooth. Add 2 oz. cointreau. Drizzle the garnish across the cake, use it as a glaze, or serve either hot or cold on the side.

Fresh Water and Love

Danielle & I in Andorra

Drafted men during my time were paid two hundred francs—the equivalency of not quite thirty-four dollars—as well as rationed twenty packs of cigarettes per month. We worked for two weeks at a time and then were allotted four days of leave, after which we would return to our positions and repeat the process. This was life. During our leave, most of us would take on any side jobs that we could find to make more money. On occasion, I would go home to visit my family or to Paris to hang out with friends. Little did I know that one of these time periods would change my life forever.

I still kept in touch with Damien and always visited with my friend on homeward bound journeys. In February of 1978, I was given a week of vacation time, and trust me, a bit of rest and relaxation was exactly what I needed. I had been saving diligently, so when Damien suggested we take a trip to Andorra, I agreed. Andorra is a beautiful little principality located right between France and Spain. Because of its location, it is the perfect melting pot of both French and Spanish cultures. Since it is situated in the midst of the Pyrenees, it is well known for hiking in the summer, as well as skiing in the winter months.

Of course, we traveled there to ski, amongst other shenanigans. Remember, we were both young men, and as you can imagine, chasing girls was high on our priority list! So, soon after we arrived in Andorra, Damien and I introduced ourselves to two beautiful ladies. I was especially interested in one of the girls—Danielle—but I was not so certain that the feeling was mutual.

Danielle was French and had trained to become a travel agent. She worked for Fram, a Toulouse based agency, but as she could speak French, Spanish, and English, the company sent her to work in Andorra. I was smitten from the moment that I first saw her. We spent as much time together as was possible that week, and it didn't take very long for me to realize that she was, in fact, quite taken with me, too.

Ahh, that week was the happiest one of my life up to that point. It was like floating on a cloud across a starry dream. We skied and walked through the village, we laughed and talked all night. We dashed into intimate, darkly lit eateries for the occasional plate of tapas or bowl of *paella*.

Danielle's company impressed me the most, I won't lie, but the *paella* was certainly delicious! It was a hearty dish that did not fail to satisfy—especially on those winter evenings. Tender rice was cooked to perfection amidst a mixture of meat, seafood, and vegetables. Olive oil and herbs like saffron and rosemary lent distinctive flavors to the dish, and overall it possessed a truly Spanish flair. Over the years, I have added my own French touches to the recipe, and I still occasionally enjoy it on a wintery Virginia night. Every time, it takes me back to that amazing week that I spent with such an amazing woman.

By the week's end, we knew that we were in love. Most every time that I was given leave, I made my way back to Andorra, and back to Danielle. I would catch a train in Paris—it was free for army men to travel by train—and ride for twelve hours to that little spot nestled in the Pyrenees. I would then take a bus to her and spend my remaining time in her arms. With only four days of leave and a full day spent on a train, on top of being young and crazy in love, each visit was over within the snap of a finger.

Leaving her to return to my duty never felt right. So, on

one particular visit, I decided to stay. I did not care about the immense heap of trouble that defection would land upon my head, or the potential jail time that desertion carried with it. I only cared about her. Two days in, my Captain, Monsieur Cardon, contacted me. Not only was he my superior, but also my friend. He recognized potential in me that I myself did not. He knew of my situation and my love for Danielle and he tracked me down to attempt to talk a bit of sense into me. I was so close to finishing my duty, and he did not want to see me throw my life away—even for love.

At great risk to himself and his own career, he had counted me present for the two extra days of my absence. This generosity came with a warning—be back for service in one day or suffer the consequences. I did not want my friend to put himself in such danger for me, and I knew that his reasoning was solid. So, as difficult as it was, I left my Danielle, boarded a train, and finished out my service.

Monsieur Cardon never allowed me to forget my actions, yet I served out the remainder of my time essentially unscathed. My draft came to an end at the beginning of June. I could have made the army my career and signed on for three or even five more years of service. But, I would not have been able to continue on as a pastry chef, and I most certainly did not wish to play with guns. I moved on along a different path, instead.

I was grateful for this portion of my journey. I learned so much—about pastry, about food, and about myself. And I learned that true love was not just something written about in fairytales. It was the most important knowledge I would ever receive.

Two and a half years later, Danielle and I would become husband and wife. That period of time would not pass without its own set of hardships, but I will save that for another story. Thirty-five more years have certainly seen their fair share of difficulties, as well as joys. To this day, Danielle and I laugh and smile when we think back upon our first week together in Andorra. She says that we lived off of fresh water and love then—*vivre d'amour et d'eau fraiche*. I completely agree.

PAELLA

serves 8

ingredients:

2 lbs. chorizo
2 red onions, diced
6 red bell peppers
saffron
salt & pepper
12 small tomatoes, diced
1 head fresh garlic
1 lbs. calamari
2 lbs. mussels

1 lbs. shrimp
2 lbs. chicken thigh
2 lbs. arborio rice
4 lbs. chicken broth
1 cup olive oil
1 cup cognac
2 cups green peas

directions:

1. Sautee, in olive oil, the chorizo, onions, bell pepper, add saffron, and tomatoes. season with salt and pepper.
2. Add the cognac and flambé.
3. Separately, add the rice and the chicken broth to a very large pot. Add all of the sauteed vegetables. cook on medium-high heat
4. During this time, sautee the chicken until caramelized. Add the chicken to the rice and vegetables, and cook for 15-20 minutes.
5. Add the calamari, mussels, add shrimp, and peas, and cook for an additional 15-20 minutes.

No. 22
Let Them Eat Steak

My year in the army ended with the beginning of a new summer season in France. I did not want to go back home to my father and his bakery. I had broken myself free from that routine and the dark path that was associated with it. But I needed work. Danielle and I were still very much in love, and I pondered moving to Andorra until an old friend came up with a very lucrative plan.

Damien moved on from my father's employment around this time, so he was in need of work, as well. We had kept in close contact throughout my year in the army, and we already knew that we worked well together. He had heard of a bakery that would pay two thousand dollars per month each plus room and board for four months because they desperately needed seasonal employees. And this bakery was located in the lovely seaside resort town of Soulac-sur Mer!

Now you must understand, back in the late 70s, two thousand dollars a month was a lot of money—especially to two young men in transition. And the draw of living right in the middle of the sun and fun for three months was beyond tempting. I envisioned walking on the beach at sunset on my days off with my lovely Danielle by my side. I was sold!

At this time, a handshake was the same as signing a contract, as most people were only as good as their word. Damien and I came to the bakery in early June and signed on as pastry chefs. We were prepared to work hard, play even harder, expected a decent bed, and decent food. We definitely worked hard, yet the rest of our expectations were nonexistent.

Damien and I did not know what we were getting into,

évidemment! The smoke and mirrors of big money and big fun hid the truth of reality. Seven days a week from six p.m. until six a.m. the following morning, we slaved away. On average, we made between four and five thousand croissants per night. And this was only the assigned duty for our side of the bakery. There were fifteen total people who worked in the bakery—all with various tasks. Our employer worked us all to death!

Damien and I would leave from our shift and spend an hour or two at most on the beach before heading back to eat and sleep. We knew that we should rest for our upcoming shift, but I suppose it was our form of rebellion. We were determined to find a tiny bit of enjoyment to cling to so that we could make it through the rest of our day. When we were on the beach, we could pretend that we were vacationing like all of the others.

We would return home to hard beds and even harder food to digest. The baker's wife cooked all of our meals, and her disposition was as tasteless as her food. One day, a couple of months into our service, we arrived back to our dormitory after a particularly tough shift. All of the seasonal workers that were housed along with us were already sitting at the community dining room table. We all took our meal at around ten that morning. Damien and I weren't looking forward to the meal, but we were both starving and exhausted. We wanted to finish our food quickly and head straight up to bed.

Our plates were especially lackluster that morning. One bland chicken neck and two boiled potatoes were all to be had. I cringed. I had never eaten this poorly in my whole life. I longed for the army's kitchen that I had just left, or even my mother's home cooking. My temper began to boil the way those potatoes had only moments before. I'd had enough.

I told the baker's wife that our meal was unacceptable. She looked at me as if to say, "There's nothing that you can do about it. Sit down and eat." In the army, I had been taught to respect your superiors, even in the most difficult of situations. I don't know if it was the exhaustion or the hunger talking, but I refused to eat that meal.

As I got up to leave the table, I spoke boldly, "Tell your husband that if Damien and I don't get a nice steak on our plates tomorrow, I won't work the following day!" I am guessing that the others at the table were just as frustrated and disgusted as I was, because four others made the very same claim. The baker's wife was shocked.

I made my way up to bed, and worked my shift later that evening without saying a word regarding the matter. My evening was just like any other, and as usual, Damien and I had our fun on the beach following our shift. I smiled when we arrived back to the house that following morning. We all had thick, juicy steaks on our plates.

To this day, I still cringe at the thought of the meal that finally sent me over the edge. Needless to say, I will not be sharing a recipe for chicken necks! However, in the region of France where my wife is from, they prepare a delicious gooseneck sausage recipe that is worthy of sharing.

The bone of the gooseneck is sliced away and discarded, and the skin of the neck is used as a casing for a delectable sausage mixture. Earthy mushrooms, shallots, herbs breadcrumbs, and seasonings are gently folded into *foie gras*. The stuffing then chills overnight for the flavors to meld before being piped into the gooseneck casing. Next, it is simmered low and slow in a pan of stock. The result is the most tender and flavorful sausage you will ever consume.

The months that I spent in Soulac-sur Mer were so very different than what I was originally expecting. Nowadays, there are labor laws in effect that prevent employers from taking advantage of their employees in such a manner. As difficult as those moths were, though, I walked away with some lessons from that part of my journey. I learned the difference between ambition and greed. I learned the importance of taking proper care of my employees. I learned to stand up for myself and others. And, most importantly, I learned that I could not stand chicken necks!

gooseneck sausage

ingredients:
- ½ cup milk
- ½ cup fresh bread
- 4 oz. pork belly
- 2 oz. fresh chanterelle mushrooms
- 4 oz. goose liver
- 4 oz. veal top round, ground
- 4 oz. goose meat
- 1 shallot
- ½ stalk celery
- 1 clove garlic
- salt, pepper, nutmeg
- 1 egg
- 1 qt. chicken broth

Directions:
1. ~~Carefully scrape~~ carefully remove skin from goose neck so as not to damage it. Turn the skin inside out and scrape away the fat, then return it to its original shape.
2. Soak the bread ~~crumbs~~ in the milk. Run the pork belly through a meat grinder with the mushrooms, celery, shallot, garlic, and goose liver.
3. Combine the ground mixture with the veal and soggy bread, excess moisture having been squeezed out. Mix well and run entire mixture through meat grinder once more.
4. Mix in the egg and then season to taste with salt, pepper, and nutmeg.
5. Fill the gooseneck with the mixture. Tie both ends with a string like sausage. Puncture in several places to prevent bursting. Place in boiling chicken broth, then reduce heat and cook, covered, on low heat for 1 hour. Slice and serve.

No. 23
Ville Lumière

Mine & Danielle's engagement party

In late summer, my brief time period in Soulac-sur Mer thankfully drew to a close, and yet again, my path in life changed. This time, I headed in a more familiar direction. With stuffed pockets and a head full of wisdom, I returned home to my father's bakery. I wonder what it is about home that somehow always draws you back?

Danielle and I were still very much in love, and the distance between us was heartbreaking. To remedy this, in the fall, she moved to my hometown so that we could be together on a full-time basis. She found employment in the Tourist Information Center in Tours and lived with Damien's parents, as my own parents were too traditional to allow us to reside under the same roof without being married. Ahh, but we both soon grew tired of our circumstances.

Working for my father became tense, once more, and Danielle and I were both ready for a change of pace. That golden city, Paris—*ville lumière*—called out to us. Very soon after, we answered her call. Many people think Paris is called "The City of Lights" because of the lampposts that line the streets and cast their warm, inviting glow. This could be farther from the truth. Its actual translation, in fact, is "City of Enlightenment" due to its culture and learning. Whatever you wish to call it, it meant freedom for Danielle and me.

In Paris, we could only afford a cheap motel room in the seedy part of town. It was so second-rate that we had to go downstairs to get water or use the restroom. I used the money that I made in Soulac-sur Mer to pay for our rent and board and to buy us a junky car. With it, we explored the city and dreamed. It may sound awful to you, but to us, it was thrilling. We were young, in love, and out on our own.

In the midst of this time, Damien came through for me, yet again. He had not returned to work for my father after we left Soulac-sur Mer, and had instead moved immediately to Paris. He led me to a certain Monsieur Pelotte, who was one of the top pastry chefs in Paris and the owner of three bakeries in the nearby suburb of Nanterre. One bakery produced bread, another produced pastry, and the third was used for sales of both. The Monsieur was looking for someone knowledgeable in pastry, and with a handshake, I was hired.

Danielle found a job with the Monsieur, as well. I insisted upon this with her, because if we were to be together, she needed to learn the ins and outs of bakery life. She worked a front of the house position in the third bakery, and was a quick study. The Monsieur was a good, fair man, and very traditional. Even so, he provided us with a small bedroom above the bakery. We said goodbye to our cheap motel room and shed no tears at doing so.

We worked hard for the Monsieur, and began to make good money. On late Sunday afternoons and Mondays—our time off—we also explored and became introduced to Paris. We discovered the real Paris, not just what you see in pictures. *Ville lumière*, indeed! Life was good.

The Monsieur was even more strict than he was traditional. He had a certain way of doing things, and insisted that we all adhere to his instruction and organization. Close to the holiday season, he showed me the special way that he created the Bûche de Noel. I remembered this intricate cake from the early days of my youth. My mother learned to make the very same cake so many years ago in her initial pastry days.

The delicate, thin, yellow sponge cake was frosted with a decadent chocolate buttercream and rolled, jelly roll style, into a log. It was then frosted on the outside with more of the buttercream and decorated to resemble an actual log. Cakes like these were true works of art, and are still wildly popular today. I fill many orders for them around the holidays at Our Daily Bread.

I appreciated the Monsieur's method, but it was very time consuming. As I worked, I recognized certain places where shortcuts could be made. These saved time, but did nothing to alter the end product. I was producing this cake much faster than the average, and this did not go unnoticed by the Monsieur. He asked those around me, "How does Thierry do this so quickly?" but was never fully satisfied with their responses, so one day, he came peering over my shoulder.

He grilled me on my own methods for producing the Bûche de Noel. I could not lie to him, so I explained how I crafted the lovely dessert. I could see frustration and elation at war on his face as I spoke. It was obvious that he was overjoyed by the fact that I could produce the same quality of product in less time. However, he was quite annoyed—not only that I had strayed from his instruction, but that he had not thought of my shortcuts first. He stomped away without another word.

Monsieur Pelotte had never called me "Chef" up until this point, regardless of how hard I had worked for him or how many delectable creations that I had produced. Yet, on this day, I earned both his respect and the title. From this day forward, no longer was I referred to simply as Thierry Tellier, but as Chef Tellier. I was humbled.

Buche de Noel

French genoise:

ingredients:

4 eggs   .27 lbs. ~~butter~~ flour

.27 lbs. sugar   1 oz. butter, melted & at Room temperature

Directions:

1. separate egg whites from Yolks. Whip the yolks. separately, whip the whites with the sugar to create meringue, or until it reaches a medium peak. fold the Yolks and flour into the meringue. Once folded, add butter.

2. Line a sheet tray with sprayed or greased parchment paper. Pour batter evenly over the pan, to fill the corners. It should be about 1/2" thick. Bake at 340°F until golden brown — 8 to 12 minutes.

3. Remove from oven and coat lightly with powdered sugar. spread a towel over the cake, then flip the pan over, guiding the cake out of the pan while holding the towel and parchment paper. leave cake on towel until needed.

mousse:

ingredients:

1 1/2 lbs. heavy cream

.15 lbs. dark chocolate

Frangelico simple syrup →

FRANGELICO SIMPLE SYRUP:

5 oz. water + 2.5 oz. sugar + 2 oz. Frangelico

→ combine all and boil. Once boiling, Remove from heat.

Directions:

1. Melt the chocolate in the microwave, using 30-second intervals and stirring in between. Whip the cream to a soft peak. Add 1/4 of the cream to the chocolate while continuously whipping. Add 1 egg yolk, whip it in, then add another 1/4 of the cream, still whipping. continue until all has been combined.

* Save the simple syrup for the next step!

assembly:

Remove the parchment paper from the genoise. Coat the entire surface with the Frangelico simple syrup, then spread half of the mousse across the cake. Roll the cake into a log, using the towel to gently press down. Do not roll the towel into the cake. Once rolled, drizzle any leftover syrup on top. Use the rest of the mousse to frost the cake. You can use your hands to frost it — your fingers will help give it a good log texture.

Garnish with shaved chocolate and powdered sugar, and any other decorations you desire.

No. 24
Dinner with the Boss

As I told you before, Monsieur Pelotte was a very strict and traditional man. This was especially evident by the way that he ran his business. Only males worked in the back with him, and only females, such as Danielle, worked in the front of the house. Although bakeries are run much differently now—like mine, for instance—this was his way, and all of his employees respected it and him. He treated us with equal respect and was dedicated to our success, as well as to the success of his business overall.

He paid us by check on a weekly basis, and we were also paid cash tips based on our performance for the week. He had a big bucket of cash sitting by his desk when we each came into the office individually to receive our compensation. He would hand you your check first, then stare down his nose past his glasses to size you up. After this, he would proceed—without looking away from you—to reach his hand into the bucket of money.

If you met or exceeded his expectations, you were compensated well from the bucket. If you did not, you very soon recognized it. He would count out the bills, quickly at first, then ever the more slowly as he reached the end. It was a game to him, I believe. Although he sat there stone faced, I feel certain that he enjoyed watching us squirm around as we hoped for at least one more bill.

Monsieur Pelotte was a watchdog when it came to cleanliness. He demanded his bakery be spotless, both front and back. It never worked if we rushed our duties or tried to slide anything past him. He always brought it to our attention. Many a day, he would ask me if I had cleaned above the doors, to which I would always reply, "*Oui,* Chef," even though I knew that I had not. He would remark, "Ah *vraiment?*" then run his finger along the top of the door facing. When it came back dirty, the look on his face spoke volumes. I would hang my head and reach for a rag.

Though he was meticulous and stern when it came to his business, he was also generous and respectful of his employees. I will not lie, his bakery was one of the top places I have ever worked for—and I have had many employers in my *la folie* forty. His generosity even extended to the quality of room and board that he provided to us all. There were no chicken necks or cold, flavorless potatoes to be found here—*mais non!*

The Monsieur's maid, Margarida, was a warm, beautiful Portuguese woman, and an excellent cook. She provided our meals through the week, and they were delicious without fail, but Sunday's dinner was always special. We only worked half a day on Sunday, as I previously mentioned. At dinnertime, we all ate together, like a large, extended family.

Monsieur Pelotte sat at the head of a huge, rustic table, and all of the men sat at this table with him. Madame Pelotte perched at a less grandiose side table with all of the lady employees. I must warn you that a whole novel could be written about the complexities of the Madame's personality—especially her temper, her airs and her graces. I won't go into how she once threw a pan of freshly made *petit fours* on the floor, simply because she did not like the way they were decorated. At Sunday dinner, though, she meekly followed her husband's instruction.

The Monsieur always served himself first, and he expected us to sample every one of the delectable dishes that were set forth upon the table. It was a mark of respect for us that we were provided with the very same meal as the boss and nothing inferior. So, he demanded that we show respect to him for such provision, as well as to his wife, and his maid, for her labor.

One Sunday in particular, Margarida had prepared a succulent leg of lamb accompanied by butter beans. The scent of the lamb tiptoed past my nose as I walked through the dining room door, and the smell immediately made my taste buds water. Margarida had added the lamb, fresh garlic and herbs together in a pan, covered the pan with foil, and had roasted the meat in the oven at a low temperature—for seven hours. The tender, roasted meat paired with the creaminess of the fresh beans was a perfect match.

We were all looking forward to a meal of such caliber— all of us except for one, that is. After the Monsieur served himself, the dishes were passed, and the rest of the plates were filled. As he looked down the table, the Monsieur noticed one man had not sampled any of the lamb. Upon being queried, the man voiced that he did not care for lamb and wished to pass on it.

In a low, controlled voice that silenced all with its power, the Monsieur politely told the man to collect his things and leave. His services were no longer required at the bakery. The man—and the rest of us, for that matter— was incredulous at first. When he realized the Monsieur was serious, the man excused himself from the table, collected his things, and left, just as he was told. It was important to respect the Monsieur, his generosity, and his table. From that moment on, and at every Sunday dinner thereafter, each person sampled every dish that was placed on the table without question.

I learned a great deal from Monsieur Pelotte in my time at his bakery. I learned new, exciting pastries and methods that I would carry with me throughout the span of my life. I learned the importance of cleanliness in the workplace, to be structured, but fair, in running a business, and that respect was of the utmost importance in any relationship. And, above all these, I learned that Sunday dinner with the boss was not to be taken lightly.

leg of lamb

Ingredients:
4-5 lbs. leg of lamb
4 tbsp. mustard, whole grain
1 sprig rosemary
2 tbsp. olive oil
1 lbs. garlic, no less than
salt, pepper, coriander to taste

directions:
1. Cover lamb with olive oil, seasonings, and mustard.
2. Line a pan with tin foil, then parchment paper over it. Place the lamb on top. Cover it with the whole garlic.
3. Lift the foil to wrap the lamb in it. Wrap it so it is airtight. Cook at 280° F for 5 hours.
4. Open the foil and serve with mashed potatoes or fresh butterbean

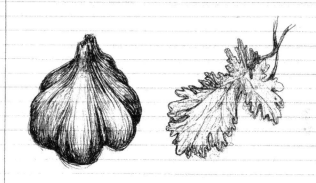

93

No. 25
The Beginning of the End

I asked Danielle to marry me in the car one day on the drive back to Paris. It was just a random Monday—our day off from Monsieur Pelotte's—when we were heading back to start a new workweek. We had returned home to Tours the Sunday afternoon before to visit with my parents. Just something about the way she looked sitting in the passenger seat of the car struck me that day. I knew I wanted to see her sitting right there for the rest of my life. So, as you say, I popped the question.

She knew I wasn't the traditional type of guy to get down on one knee to propose. Even so, she was surprised at my timing. After her initial shock was over, she said yes. I've been grateful that she did for the past thirty-five years. On July 5, 1980—almost a year and a half after we met—we were married.

Danielle and I loved our lives in Paris, but we had been getting along rather well with my parents. The fact that we had gotten married pleased them so they invited and welcomed us back home. My father wished to open a fourth bakery. He had been eyeing a property that housed a covered market, and he wanted to place a bakery inside the small building that was attached to the market. He even offered Danielle a job there. She was thrilled because she loved the look of the property and the idea of the concept. The decision was final. We moved back to Tours.

It was like a dream come true. My father and I were finally working together side by side and getting along. My mother took care of the finances, Danielle ran the front of the house in the new bakery, and I oversaw the production. Even my sister joined in on the organization side of the business. It was now a genuine family affair. In the years that we spent there, I acquired another bakery of my own, we procured three mobile trucks with which to sell our wares, and Danielle gave birth to our son, Franck. *La vie était belle*—life was, indeed, good.

In the midst of this prosperity, my father bought a farm. He had grown up on a farm, and had always wished to own one. It was rather large—two hundred fifty acres, to be exact—and he raised one thousand lambs, and harvested fruit, vegetables, and herbs. My mother also tended to rabbits and chickens. As the farm was a time-consuming project, my father stepped away from the bakeries and left the overseeing of them completely in my hands.

Mom, Dad & Franck on the farm

At first, I was overjoyed at his confidence in me. I also loved bringing my little family to visit the farm. I took Franck fishing there on my father's rather large pond, and my son also found great pleasure in playing with the ducks. Many times, my father and I would also go duck hunting together. And occasionally after our visits, if my mother had slain and cleaned a rabbit or two, my family would stay for dinner. Mother would prepare a scrumptious rabbit with mustard sauce that was well worth staying for.

Mother sautéed the rabbit in butter along with shallots, garlic, and a lovely white Vouvray wine. She would then allow the mixture to reduce on low while she prepared a Dijon mustard and cream sauce. This would eventually be drizzled on top of the rabbit. It was a beautiful dish.

The succulent rabbit was seared to perfection on the outside, and fork tender, it dripped with juice on the inside from the slow reduction. The meat was infused with the crisp flavor of the wine, and the garlic and shallots perfumed the rabbit while providing a tender accompaniment. The sinfully luscious mustard cream pushed the dish over the top. I'm sure you now recognize why we eagerly joined my parents for this meal.

These visits to the farm were wonderful. I finally had the relationship with my father that I had always wanted, and I was able to share such bounty with my son. Ahh, but circumstances change just like the wind. Isn't that always the case? As time progressed, the relationship with my father again began to deteriorate. The solitude of the farm did not suit him, and his life sadly spiraled farther and farther down a bad path. The hectic pace of bakery life and running his multiple bakeries favored my father. I will admit, it does the same for me, today. I am that much my father's son.

With the snap of his fingers, the work environment also changed for the worse. My father became ever more difficult to deal with, and money was suddenly disappearing. One day, out of the complete blue, my father showed up and fired me on the spot. He gave no explanation for his actions. We were all stunned.

I was angered at this, but resolved to run the lone bakery that I had acquired on my own, and support my family. Alas, this was not to be. Three days after I was fired, my own bakery burnt to the ground. I never learned the cause. Perhaps it was because the machinery was unaccustomed to supporting so much production. At any rate, my insurance did not cover the fire, and my father refused to help. Both he—and our relationship—had gone off the deep end. Just like that, my alliance with my father and my livelihood were both gone.

I was desolate, but I had a wife and a young son to care for. I sifted through the ashes and came up with a plan. I took my car keys, my business keys, and my ownership documentation and left them on the counter at my father's newest bakery. Every material thing that I owned now belonged to him. I locked the door behind me and never looked back. In fact, the only thing that I salvaged from this time in my life was Mother's rabbit recipe.

rabbit in mustard sauce

Ingredients:

3 tbsp. olive oil

4 saddle of rabbit

1 onion

4 cloves garlic

2 ribs celery

1 medium carrot

1 cup white wine — preferably chardonnay

1 qt. cream

3 tbsp. whole grain mustard

2 cups chicken broth

salt & pepper, to taste

4 bay leaves

Directions:

1. Preheat oven to 350° F. Heat olive oil in a sauté pan. Sear the rabbit until golden brown on both sides. Remove from pan and place in 9x13" baking pan. Drain all but 1 tbsp. oil.

2. Add the onion, garlic, celery, and carrot. Cook on medium-high heat for 15 minutes, stirring frequently.

3. Add the mustard, stirring to combine. Then add the white wine and reduce by half.

4. Add the cream, chicken broth, bay leaves, and a pinch of salt and pepper. Bring to a boil, then simmer for 15 minutes.

5. Pour the sauce over the rabbit. Cover with foil and bake at 350° for one hour. Remove from oven and check for tenderness. Meat should almost fall off the bone. Let sit for 10 minutes. Serve over rice or pasta.

Welcome to the Family

Danielle's Parents

After my father's inexplicable behavior and the destruction of our only source of income, Danielle, Franck, and I found refuge at the home of Danielle's parents. We had no money and honestly, no choice. The peace of their home and their hospitality was such a change from what we had just been through. Danielle and I met these with enthusiasm, because we were beyond grateful.

While we had dated, Danielle and I had not visited with her parents for lengthy durations, as they did not care for our living arrangement. They were very traditional, like many of their generation. After we were married, and especially in this instance, they were extremely supportive and welcomed us with open arms.

So much so, that upon our arrival, they insisted on preparing a "Welcome to the Family" lunch for me. We let them know that we did not wish to impose, but they would not take no for an answer. They planned to cook me a lovely steak lunch, and I could see the joy in their eyes. How could I refuse?

You must understand that France is very much like other countries, such as America, in that each region is known for consuming certain styles of cuisine. Like you would recognize New York for pizza or North Carolina for barbecue, the southwest of France is known for lamb, veal, duck, goose, guinea hens, and the like. Danielle's family consumed very little red meat. But her parents knew this was not the case in my region. My father insisted that we eat red meat at one meal or another every day except Sunday, when my mother prepared her prized roasted chicken. In offering to cook steak for me, it was yet another way for Danielle's parents to welcome me into their home.

My little family became situated in Danielle's old room and freshened up while lunch was being prepared. When we sat down to the table, Danielle's mother served us with a gleaming smile. She was so proud of her accomplishment that we beamed in return. When the steak was plated, we began to smile for a much different reason.

Danielle's mother had prepared beef *tournedos*, which are small, round, filet-style cuts of beef that are sliced from the end of the tenderloin. I was accustomed to a thicker, much larger ribeye-style cut of steak, and so the meat on my plate appeared to be like toddler-sized food. Danielle could not stop laughing! Her parents were confused by her mirth, until she explained that the steaks that I typically consumed were more than four times the size of the one that currently rested on my plate. I could sense their embarrassment, so I reassured them that it was a lovely cut of meat, and I could not wait to sample it. But, I must say, I was still hungry when I pushed away from the table.

Danielle's parents helped us to get a small place to stay for a couple of months until we could figure out our next move. We shared many meals with them in our time there. Honestly, once I became familiar with the food in the southwest of France, I became a bigger fan of it than that of which I grew up eating. The fare was lighter, and the flavors were exquisite. Red meat is hearty and sustaining, *certainement,* but sampling the foods of the southwest was like opening a new door for me with regards to cuisine.

I fell in love with pan-seared *foie gras* with figs. Danielle's mother was a master at preparing this. The fattened goose liver was rich and buttery, and the added snap of the figs lent a sweet depth to the dish. It was truly a work of art, and every bite was a treasure for the palate to behold.

I still cherish the time that we spent with Danielle's parents. We drew even closer as a family because we took the time to truly get to know one another. It brought my heart great joy to watch them interact with Franck. And Danielle simply glowed every time that she showed me around her lovely little village. It was a time to recharge, replenish our souls, and rethink our goals. I will be forever grateful.

foie gras & figs

ingredients:

1 tbsp. butter
4 slices foie gras ea., at ½" thick
6 ea. fresh figs, halved
1 ea. shallots, minced
2 tbsp. honey

2 oz. cognac
1 oz. port wine
salt & pepper, to taste
nutmeg, as needed

directions:

1. Place foie gras in freezer until very chilled, but not frozen.
2. Place 4 slices of foie gras on a cutting board. Using a small, sharp knife, score the pieces, no more than 1/16" deep. Season with salt, pepper, and nutmeg. Return to freezer until ready to use.
3. In a medium sauté pan, melt 1 tbsp. butter over high heat. Once melted, place figs cut-side-down and cook until slightly caramelized. Add the shallots and sauté for 2 minutes, shaking the pan to loosen the figs.
4. Pull the pan off the stove, then add the port wine, cognac, and honey. Return the pan to the stove, being cautious as the liquor will ignite. Cook until liquid thickens to a syrup consistency. Season with salt and pepper. Remove, and hold in container until needed.
5. Put a small sauté pan on very high heat, until almost smoking. Place the foie gras, scored side down, and sear for 30 seconds on each side. Carefully remove from pan and place on paper towel.
6. Serve each plate with sauce and 3 pieces of fig.

No. 27
Dating My Wife

I am of the mindset that to keep a marriage alive and the *amour* flowing, every now and again you must "date" your wife. After all, a happy wife equals a happy life! Danielle and I had quite a few lovely "dates" while we resided with her parents. Not only did we now have a bit of time freed up, we also had trusted care for Franck. We would explore around Danielle's village and beyond and revel in the opportunities to spend alone time together. It was beautiful.

Danielle hiking in Pyrenees

We took advantage of the fair climate, and hiked extensively throughout the Pyrenees. On one of those hikes, we discovered a beautiful lake—Lac d'Aumar. The lake was pristine and crystal clear. On some days, I would bring a fishing pole along because I could catch truly wild trout there. The fish was known locally as *salmon fontaine*, and it was simply divine when pan seared with almonds. Lac d'Aumar instantly became our favorite, and we spent much time there soaking up the scenery and drowning in each other. That lake is still dear to our hearts—so much so that in our wills we have designated that after we pass, our ashes are to be scattered there.

As much as we enjoyed the outdoors, hiking, and the lake, we truly adored visiting the village's outdoor market. Danielle had spent her whole life sampling treasures from the bounty that this market offered. For me, I had never seen anything like it before. I was amazed! This market was the real deal, and it put to shame similar outdoor markets in my region.

The market was covered with an elaborate and

extensive roof. Small vendor's tables lined both the right and left sides of the space, and each vendor was so friendly and welcoming. Even strangers who perused the market struck up random conversations. Such was not the case in my region, and at first I did not know what to make of it. But my sweet Danielle was just as warm and open toward anyone she met. In time, this beautiful character trait of hers rubbed off on me.

The market was extremely popular with the locals, neighboring villages, and traveling visitors, alike. We had to creatively weave throughout to be able to view each vendor's wares. Everything fresh and tempting could be found there—whatever your heart desired. Fresh flowers, vegetables, meat and poultry, herbs, cheeses, *saucisson*— the offerings appeared to be limitless. The farm to table mentality was vibrant and alive at this market.

I was always tempted by the booths of vegetables that had been picked at the height of ripeness and perfection. My mouth also watered when we passed tables of plump, fresh squab. This young pigeon's meat was succulent, and its flavor reminded me of the dark portion of chicken. Paired with fresh, sweet green peas, this little bird tempted the senses with its aromatic, juicy flavor. And the tender leaves and vines that suspended the peas were not only lovely when garnishing the plate, but added a nice crunch when consumed.

As for Danielle, she was enamored with the cheese. A particular man made his cheese from scratch, and sold it at the market. It was heavenly. Had we not been so in love, I might have become worried that she would leave me for the cheese man. His cheese was that tempting, *absolument!* The market had always been open for business on Thursday afternoons, and Danielle and her friends never missed a single Thursday. It was both a trip and a real treat for them.

Danielle's favorite cheese was the greuile. It was made from sheep's milk, as they were predominantly raised in the area. To make the greuile, the milk was heated until the curds and the whey separated. The whey, or liquid, was reduced—heavily. This formed a very soft, luscious, fatty cheese. It was very difficult to make, or so we were told. Eaten with honey or chives, it did not matter—it was just as delicious.

I had never truly experienced cheese before I was introduced to this man's genius. I have sampled many appetizing cheeses throughout my life, but none have compared to his offerings. Many years later, Danielle and I would find this same man in exactly this same spot selling exactly the same cheeses. And, yes, they were just as scrumptious as we remembered.

SQUAB & FRESH GREEN PEAS

· serves 2 ·

ingredients:

1 whole squab or dove, cut in 4	8 oz. chicken stock
3 shallots, diced	1 bunch fresh parsley
1 clove garlic, minced	1 large carrot, diced
1 cup white wine	1 lbs. fresh green peas
2 bay leaves	4 oz. pancetta, diced
salt & pepper	4 oz. butter

directions:

1. Sautée squab or dove with butter, salt, pepper, garlic, pancetta, carrot, and shallots.
2. cover with white wine. cook for 20 minutes.
3. Add green peas, chicken stock, and bay leaves. cook for an additional 25-30 minutes.
4. serve. The meat is good to serve pink, if desired.

No. 28
The Island Way

After staying with Danielle's parents for a couple of months, a new path revealed itself to me. I found out that a job was available on the island of Martinique. This was a completely new direction for us, and well out of our comfort zone. But, as grateful as we were to Danielle's parents and as much as I had taken away from our time with them, a change of course was exactly what we needed.

We said our goodbyes to family and friends. I left the southwest of France with even more respect for Danielle's parents. Honestly, I believe they felt the same toward me. With full hearts, my little family and I surrendered to the island's call. It was the first time that we would make a drastic move of this caliber, but you will see, it would not be the last.

At age twenty-seven, with my wife and young son beside me, we left all that was comfortable and familiar and made the island of Martinique our home. It was like a whole new world, compared to where we had come from. The culture, the pace, and the people were all very different. Living on "island time" was something that I was certainly unaccustomed to.

I found work immediately, but it was just a way to support my family and me. There was no *joie de vivre* to be found in that position—no joy of living. I made new connections, though, that would prove rather fruitful. Monsieur Gateau and Monsieur San Pare were two local businessmen who made my acquaintance. Monsieur Gateau's parents had been bakers, and Monsieur San Pare was a food importer who resold the food he acquired on the island.

Me and Monsieurs Gateau & San Pare

These business partners offered me a position as a pastry chef at their establishment. After careful scrutiny on my part, I did not prefer the way they ran their business. I told them no thank you and prepared to stick with my current employment until a new opportunity arose. These men would not take no for an answer. They liked the fire and spark that they recognized in my personality, and after a bit of conferring between the gentlemen, a new offer was presented. It was one that I could not refuse.

The partners offered to open a bakery and give me the free reign of overseeing and managing it. They would front the capital, and I would take care of the rest. It was almost like having my very own shop. Since I had no start-up money of my own, this offer dazzled me, and I agreed on the spot.

When they said I would take care of all of the details, did they ever mean it. The site for the shop needed a complete makeover. I tiled the floor, painted the walls, cleaned the oven, and set up the interior. The property was transformed into the perfect little shop.

There were many challenges, as there always are when opening a brand new business. The largest challenge of all was the oven. It was a wood-burning oven, and I had never cooked bread on one such as this. It took a bit of a learning curve, and some creativity, but soon I mastered its use. I began to create delectable food, bread, and pastries and the business flourished, much to my delight—as well as that of the Monsieurs! In fact, this is the very shop where my former general's wife, Madame Gagnard, reconnected both with me and her beloved chocolate confection, my Noirmont.

I opened the shop early every day. Before the people of the island went to their jobs or the tourists went to the beach, these patrons bought my delicacies. I sold *croissants* by the dozens, as well as *quiche* laced with treasures of the sea. Conch was both delicious and readily available on the island. I would cook it for hours until the meat became tender. Afterward, I would combine the meat with pimientos, onions, and habaneros. I would then smother handmade dough with this concoction, pour the mixture of egg, milk, and seasoning—known as the liquid—on top of this, and bake the *quiche* until both the top and the crust became golden brown.

Ahh, the aroma of the *quiche* as it baked fragranced the shop and drew in customers like the song of a siren. The buttery, flaky crust and the creamy, delicate egg were enhanced by the sweetness of the conch. Add in the perfect amount of heat from the habaneros and the earthy, savory onions and pimientos, and the dish caressed the palate with flavor. Sometimes, I would replace the conch with chunks of sweet lobster. The end result was just as favorable, and I sold out of these treats every time they were made available.

I will not lie to you. The move to Martinique was not an easy transition for my family. With time, however, we made our mark on the island and built quite a good life for ourselves. We worked hard, as always, but enjoyed the sea and all of the benefits of island living. We hit upon quite the treasure in August of 1986 when our daughter, Aurore, was born. Our family was growing and thriving, and Danielle and I could not have been more joyful.

Deep down, I longed to be the director of my own destiny. After two years of living on the island and working for Monsieurs Gateau and San Pare, I offered to buy the bakery. They pondered the idea, but ultimately did not accept my offer. They wanted our arrangement to remain as it already stood. I simply could not go agree to it. The desire to call the shop—any shop—my own was too great.

As much as I hated to do so, the Monsieurs and I parted ways. To make ends meet, I took on a job managing the bread production for a local grocery store. I worked there for six months, but I was not happy. I still yearned to own my own bakery, once more.

The vacation was over for me. The island way no longer brought me joy. Danielle and I decided to return to France and begin a new search for another bakery to call our own. Little did we know the choices that would be presented or the direction our family would be led—all because of that search.

lobster Quiche

Ingredients:

1 ea. deep dish 9" pie shell
5 oz. lobster meat, cooked
1/4 cup parsley, chopped
4 Large eggs
1 cup milk
1 cup heavy cream

1/2 tsp. ground nutmeg
1/4 tsp. celery seed
1/4 tsp. ground coriander
1 tsp. salt
1/2 tsp. pepper

Directions:

1. Pre heat oven to 350°F.
2. Whisk eggs, milk, cream, & spices (including salt and pepper), until combined.
3. Place lobster meat and parsley in the pie shell. Fill the Rest with the egg/milk/cream mixture.
4. Bake for 30 minutes. Rotate the pan and bake for another 15 minutes. Check for doneness using a small knife which should come out of the Quiche clean.

No. 29
Choices

When I returned to France with my family, I had no idea what we were going to do. We had practically no money saved, and I desperately needed a job. I was certain about two things, though: 1) that I wanted to work with a wood burning oven, and 2) that I did not want to work for my father. The desire to possess my own bakery and be the maker of my own destiny still burned in the back of my mind. However, in the meantime, I had to find some sort of basic employment to provide for my family.

I began to research both locally and distant, and I came across two potential leads. The first was located in a cozy little town in the Pyrenees. A baker had walked away from his bakery, and the townspeople wanted someone skilled to run it. The mayor of the town was interviewing couples or small families in the hopes of finding the perfect match.

This option was appealing to me for three different reasons. First, no up front money was required, as the bakery was fully functioning. Second, the potential of having my own business once again could finally come to fruition. And, third, we would be close to Danielle's parents, as they lived only about an hour and a half away. If we were living in such close proximity, Danielle's parents could watch Franck and Aurore grow, as well as have an active role in all of our lives. If you haven't yet realized, I will make this clear now—family has always been and will always be extremely important to Danielle and me.

As wonderful as the first option appeared to be, another more exotic lead drew my attention, as well. An up and coming French bakery and *café* in America was in need of workers. The company already had one location in Florida and two in Texas. Wood burning ovens were used there, just like I now preferred, and the company was very supportive of bringing over and training applicants from abroad. The thought of moving to America was lofty, thrilling, and, to be honest, a bit scary. I would be dragging my family halfway across the world into the unknown. On top of that, Danielle knew English, but I was not versed in the language at all!

We had such choices to pursue. Should we stay within our comfort zone and attempt to find something close to family and friends in France? Should we interview in the little town in the Pyrenees and hope that our family was chosen to take over the abandoned bakery? Should we entertain the notion of a new life and a fresh start in America? The thoughts made my head spin. My family's well-being was on the line, whichever option I ultimately chose. There was no room for error.

Danielle and I weighed the pros and cons of each choice. She was ready for a change, and did not want to return to the drama and issues that surrounded a permanent move back to France. Quite frankly, neither did I. She had the confidence that we would succeed, no matter which choice became our final decision. After much deliberation, we resolved to leave the selection in fate's hands.

We traveled to the Pyrenees and interviewed with the mayor of the town. The tiny bakery was simply adorable, and Danielle and I fell in love with the quaint mountain village that surrounded it and the promise of a simple life. Aulus-les-Bains was named and known for its thermal, spa-like water. It was once a very popular place, however the village had gone a bit downhill as the years had passed and its population had dwindled. But it was still a lovely environment, and we could envision ourselves living a happy life there.

Just outside the village, we came across a charming little restaurant where we stopped for a brief rest and lunch. The kind woman who ran the establishment recognized that we were new to the area. She chatted freely and inquired about our visit. We explained our purpose in Aulus-les-Bains, and we even went so far as to share the rest of our story and the decision that demanded our attention.

The woman gasped when we mentioned America. She and her husband had temporarily moved to the United States years before under similar circumstances. They loved it there, but made the difficult decision to move back to France. Her husband passed away shortly after their return, and she was left to run their restaurant alone. She spoke in a wistful and emotional voice as she relayed to us that she had always regretted their decision to return to France and had always wondered what the future would have held had they stayed in America.

We chatted more with the woman, finished our lunch, and prepared to leave. The conversation left a lasting impression on both Danielle and me. Was this fate's way of nudging us in the other direction? When we returned home, I indulged and sent my resume to the company in America. All that was left to do was sit back and see which option—if either—would come through.

Very soon afterward, it appeared the decision was made for us. A gentleman contacted me—let's call him Paul—who was a Loire Valley-born businessman and the founder of the American chain of cafés. He queried me as to exactly where I was from, and I was surprised to learn that his mother had been from Tours and a patron of my parents' second bakery. He offered me a job, but wanted me to come to America for a few weeks so that the company could assess my skills. I was flown to Dallas, Texas, and I was amazed at how different America was to any country I had ever witnessed.

I spent most of that time period working, and I was impressed at the organization and management of the company. The *café's* staff was certainly internationally represented. Everyone spoke a different language—French, English, Vietnamese, and Irish, just to name a few, but somehow production still flowed without a hitch.

The *café's* interior was beautiful, warm, and rustic. Rich wooden beams lined the ceiling, and those same wood tones were carried throughout the space. French Impressionist paintings lined the walls. A stone fireplace adorned with country implements was the focal point of the dining room, and a cheery fire was constantly to be kept lit in the winter months.

And the food was unlike any I had ever experienced. The *café* served breakfast, lunch, and dinner in a cafeteria-style setting. The traditional French staples and favorites—like *croissants, baguettes*, and various pastries—were present, of course, along with dishes that were both new and exciting. To many, you hardly think twice about something as simple as a Caesar salad dressed with croutons, Parmesan cheese, and the heady flavor of anchovies, yet all of this was completely new to me. I had never eaten salads such as this before, as vegetables had typically been served cooked in my region. I became instantly addicted.

Two favorites of the Dallas-based customers were the Croque-monsieu*r*, and the creamy tomato basil soup. Tender, salty ham and creamy cheese—typically Gruyere—were layered and grilled on thick, crusty bread. The sandwich was then smothered in a decadent *béchamel* sauce. Add a fried egg on top and the delicacy was transformed into a Croque-madame!

Ahh, and the soup—the acidity of the tomatoes, the sweetness of the basil, a hint of salty, freshly grated parmesan cheese, and the silky cream all swirled in the soup pot. Bowl after bowl of the luscious concoction was sold, and I understood why. I had never tasted a soup so rich and velvety. At the time, the Croque-monsieur and -madame were making their way across the world and into popular cuisine. Such a soup as this particular tomato basil was *nouveau* cuisine then, however, even though this is not the case today. Back then, the company regarded it as one of their signature dishes.

They impressed upon us that it was a recipe that would remain within the company and could not be shared. Even so, I have carried a love for it—for all of the dishes—with me down through the years. I serve both the Croque-monsieur, as well as, occasionally, the Croque-madame in my own Our Daily Bread. I have found that these make a lovely pairing with a hearty, savory, herb-infused French Onion Soup.

I was eager to continue working with the company, but Paul had run into a bit of difficulty regarding my work visa., so I returned to France where we all waited on pins and needles. Would my visa come through? Would we be moving to America? To make matters more unclear, in the meanwhile, the mayor of the homey little village in the Pyrenees informed us that our family had been chosen to take over the bakery and welcomed us with open arms. This both shocked and delighted us! Perhaps fate had a much different path in store for us?

As much as I loved the company in America, we prepared to take the mayor up on his offer. It was a sure thing, and the American option was still very much up in the air. My family needed both provision and stability. Our minds were settled. But, like a scene in a movie, that very day, Paul called. My work visa had been approved. Instantly, we were torn. Just which was the right decision?

Once again, we weighed the pros and cons. Both choices held equal draw for us. We were overjoyed, and at the same time, majorly stressed. We needed advice. That evening, we rounded up my mother, my in-laws, and a few various extended family members. We dined together and posed our dilemma to them in the hopes of a bit of guidance.

America? The majority was shocked and dismayed at the notion of us uprooting and settling so far away. Only one family member in the bunch—a wise, old uncle—spoke up. In a gravely voice, he uttered, "Go to America. You can always come back to France if you don't make it. But how will you know if you don't try?"

Danielle and I looked at each other and smiled. We were already leaning in this direction. We just needed to hear it voiced aloud. We chose to allow the call of our hearts to be our guide—not fate or any other outside source or opinion.

While the bakery in the Pyrenees promised a simple life and a safe solution, we were ready for new adventures—a new start. Through the years that would follow, especially during the hard times—and yes, life would throw plenty of those our way—we often thought about that little village in the Pyrenees and wondered what might have been.

Such is human nature. When life-defining choices are presented to us, I can't help but think that we are all guilty of this at some point or another. We discovered—many years later when we revisited the area—that soon after we had left for America the bakery in that sweet little village burnt to the ground. The bakery was never rebuilt. Remember the kind woman from the restaurant where we had originally stopped for lunch? She was still there when we visited the second time. She was the one who shared this shocking news with us. All that to say, following our hearts was the right decision, *absolument!*

Croque monsieur & French onion soup

Croque monsieur:

Ingredients:

8 slices thick-cut white bread
8 slices swiss cheese
12 oz thin-cut ham
2 cups bechemel sauce (recipe follows)
2 cups shredded mozzarella cheese

Directions:

Build sandwiches: each gets 1 slice cheese, 3 oz. ham, ½ cup bechemel sauce, ½ cup mozzarella. Cook at 350° F for 10 minutes, or until golden brown.

bechemel sauce:

Ingredients:

2 cups milk	¼ tsp. pepper
1 oz. butter	¼ tsp. nutmeg
1 oz. flour	
½ tsp. salt	

Directions:

In a small pot, melt butter over high heat with salt, pepper, and nutmeg. Once melted, add flour and whisk until it reaches a wet, sandy consistency. Add the milk and bring to a boil, stirring frequently. Lower the heat and simmer for 10 minutes. Remove from stove, transfer to a container, and refrigerate until completely cooled.

French onion soup:

Ingredients:

4 sweet yellow onions, julienne
6 cloves garlic, sliced
5 sprigs thyme
½ bunch parsley, chopped
2 bay leaves
1 cup Madeira
1 cup cognac

1 tbsp. Worcestershire sauce
4 croutons, ½" thick
2 qt. beef broth
1 cup gruyere cheese, shredded
salt & pepper, to taste

Directions:

In a 3-4 qt. sauce pot, sweat the onions and garlic over low-medium heat, until deeply caramelized. Add thyme, bay leaves, then deglaze with Madeira, cognac, and Worcestershire. Reduce by half. Add the beef broth and bring to a boil. Lower heat and simmer for 20 minutes, uncovered, or until it reduces by half. Season w/ salt and pepper.
Divide soup into four oven-safe cups. Top each with a crouton & and ¼ cup gruyere cheese. Broil until cheese is bubbly and golden brown.

Serve croque monsieur and French onion soup together.

No. 30
Coming to America

On December 12, 1988, with two trunks of possessions and $482 dollars to our name, my family and I landed in Dallas, Texas. We were grateful for the opportunity, and for the change in scenery, excited over what the future might hold, and scared—all at the same time. I was thirty years old when I reached the United States. I knew that my family and I could not keep moving from place to place forever. We had to put down roots. So, on that chilly December day when my feet touched the ground in America, I vowed to myself that, for my family's sake, I would succeed here. If I did not, though, I was resolute that I would never go back to France.

Arriving in America was mind blowing for Danielle and the children. It was not as much for me because, you will remember, I had already visited for company training. Even so, during that time, my experiences revolved around work. I suppose I *was* a bit starry-eyed myself, as well. We expected America to be nothing but skyscrapers, because that was all that we had ever seen on television. It thoroughly surprised us that the only buildings of that caliber could be found downtown, and that the city was mostly comprised of neighborhoods and smaller commercial centers.

We were intrigued at the thought that we would be living in the city that neighbored Southfork Ranch. The television program Dallas had a huge following in France. Danielle and I were friends with a particular couple who would never miss an episode. No matter the occasion, they would politely excuse themselves, dash out the door, and rush home to watch the show! We just laughed. We never understood the fascination.

Since the ranch was so close by, we decided to take a tour of it. We could share the experience with our friends in France—they would be thrilled! What a disappointment when we finally toured the house and grounds, though. We couldn't believe how television magic could transform a setting into something completely different than it actually was. My apologies, I am jumping too far forward much too quickly.

When we arrived in Dallas, we thought that our plane had taken a wrong turn and had landed instead in some sort of fairy world or at the North Pole. The whole city was decorated for Christmas, and the environment took our breath away. We stared in awe at the twinkling lights, holiday figures, shimmering colors, and overloaded trees everywhere we turned. We had never seen so many brightly wrapped packages! They spilled out from under every Christmas tree in sight. Franck was quite disappointed that there were not choirboys in flowing robes standing outside on the streets serenading the bustling crowds!

In France, we had never experienced Christmas in such a way. Electricity was far too expensive there for anyone to decorate his or her home so lavishly. Attending midnight mass, followed by *croissants* and warm drinks at home while families waited for Santa—those were our traditions. When Santa did arrive, he brought simple gifts—and fewer ones, at that—and our stockings were filled with nuts, fruits, candies, and perhaps a small trinket.

Franck, Aurore & Danielle with Santa
(my boss)

Eight days after we arrived, my new company held its annual office Christmas party. My whole family was invited, and we were both shocked and delighted at the tables of food and drink, the decorations, and the music. Again, it was like stepping into a wonderland. Franck and Aurore were excited to take their picture with Santa—who was actually my boss, Paul, in disguise.

Toward the end of the party, Paul began handing out brightly wrapped gifts to the various employees. When he made his way to me, the box that he handed me was huge! He wished us all a fond, "Merry Christmas!" and I ripped the paper off of the package. It was a brand new color television set. My jaw dropped. Stunned, I thanked him for the gift, and we left the party to head toward our home.

You see, to help my family out, Paul had generously provided a small house for us to live in until we could get on our feet. Looking back now, I understand that in Paul giving us that television set, he was simply adding on another layer of generosity. He was giving from his heart to an overwhelmed family that had come to this new world from our old world. At the time, though, I won't lie—I thought he was crazy! Once we arrived home, I told Danielle that I didn't know if I could work for a company that displayed such extravagance.

Danielle encouraged me to give everything a proper chance. She has always been the voice of reason for me, so I listened. Christmas Eve came around less than a week later. To embrace a tradition of our new homeland, we prepared turkey and mashed sweet potatoes. But, of course, we added a French twist.

The turkey breast was coated in lavender and honey and the outside was seared to give the meat a delectable crust. It was then oven-baked so the meat would retain all of its juicy tenderness. Our little house was perfumed with the smell of it. We gave mashed sweet potatoes more of an American flair by topping them with a mixture of melted butter and crushed corn flakes. But we added French thyme for a pop of flavor. These, too, went into the oven, and the topping crisped and browned from the heat. While it was certainly new for us, it was a sumptuous meal—a beautiful mix of French and American styles.

I worked hard—both to thank Paul for his help, and because working hard was in my blood. It still is. Because of my past knowledge and experience, I was a quick study. This did not go unnoticed. Approximately two months later, Paul would display his confidence in my abilities, as well as gauge my management potential by temporarily sending me to a completely new corner of this new world— New Orleans during Mardi Gras!

lavender turkey

ingredients:

4 servings organic turkey breast	1 cup butter
2 bottles light beer	3 bay leaves
fresh lavender	Herbs de Provence
1 cup honey	1 cup white wine
1 onion	1 cup veal demiglase
4 cloves garlic	1 carrot, diced
salt, pepper	1 stalk celery, diced

directions:

1. Marinate the turkey in the white wine, beer, honey, lavender, and bay leaves for 24 hours.

2. Pull the turkey from the marinade and season it with salt, pepper a pinch of herbs de provence, and more lavender. In a sauté pan, cook it in butter until lightly brown and caramelized. Transfer into a baking dish, and cook in the oven, covered, at 350° F for 1 hour or until turkey reaches 160° F.

3. Using the pan that you sauteed the turkey in, sauté the onions, garlic, carrot, and celery.

4. Using cheese cloth, strain the marinade from the first step. Add the juice into the vegetables. Reduce by half.

5. Add the demiglase to thicken the sauce. Glaze the turkey and serve.

121

No. 31
Carnival

French Market in New Orleans

My family and I had only been living in America for a couple of months when I was selected for a special assignment. Even though I possessed many years worth of knowledge and skills, I was still very much the new kid on the block when it came to American culture. So when I was told that in early February I would be filling in for the head chef in New Orleans, Louisiana, I was thrilled for the chance to explore this famous city. I was only informed about the basics: that the chef had taken leave for vacation and that I would be there for three weeks. I figured out why he had done so just as soon as I arrived there.

While my family stayed in Dallas, I reached the *café's* French Quarter location in February of 1989—right in the middle of the city's Carnival season! I had never seen anything like it. It was nuts. The chef had taken his vacation because he knew that Mardi Gras and Carnival would be crazy. Me being the new guy to the country, I did not have a clue. Yes, I had heard of Mardi Gras, but I had no idea about the shenanigans that would take place on Bourbon Street and beyond.

Carnival in New Orleans was a wild ride. The city was in twenty-four hour party mode. City workers had to even go so far as to grease the balcony posts and flagpoles every morning with petroleum jelly so that revelers would not attempt to climb them. I had seen major partying at events like La Feria—but nothing like this. I was beyond fascinated, and quite nervous.

Luckily, the company had a plan of action in place. Due to the large volume of sales that the team had to produce for, the assistants were to arrive at one a.m. to begin prep work. Because I was filling in for the head chef, I was to arrive at three a.m. I wanted to impress my superiors and prove to them that even though I was new, they had chosen the right man for the job. The whole night before my first shift, my stomach flipped with anxious butterflies. I could not sleep. As I lay in bed tossing and turning, I decided to stop fighting with the bedcovers and go in early to offer assistance.

When I arrived to a darkened *café*, those butterflies in my stomach immediately went into hyper drive. Surely the assistants had remembered to come in? I flipped on the kitchen light switches to find three assistants drunkenly asleep on the prep tables. Three more who were supposed to be in by five a.m. failed to show up at all. I was furious!

I did what was natural—what I would have done back in my own bakeries in France. I awakened the drunken men and fired them on the spot. The same fate would later await the no shows. This satisfied my rage until the realization dawned on me that I had fired all of my assistants! My wrath instantly became replaced with fear. What was I going to do?

Yet again, I did what was second nature to me: I put my head and my hands to the grindstone, and I worked. Somehow, the remaining employees and I powered through that day, except there were not nearly enough people available to cover for the assistants. Nor was there enough food produced to cash in on a city full of hungry revelers. Needless to say, the corporation was none too happy with me. *Oh non!* Thankfully, my superiors took care of the results of my over zealousness, though, and there was relatively smooth—albeit busy—sailing for the rest of my time there.

Despite the madness, I fell in love with the city. New

Orleans was laced with magic that I could feel deep in my bones. The rich history, the combination of French and Spanish architecture, the culture, the vibe, the music, and the food—I loved it all! In my downtime, I wandered all over the city, and reveled in its enchantment.

On these explorations, a man who worked for my company showed off all of the hotspots in the city. This man helped me discovered the city's most famous *café*. The warm, airy *beignets* drowned in powdered sugar that they served were distinctly French. I had eaten similar treats many times in France. Their *café au lait* tasted of chicory, and as the flavor hit my palate, I was immediately transported back to my childhood.

I sampled many Creole and Cajun dishes as I traversed the city with my companion. Hearty red beans and rice livened with salty Tasso and served alongside fat Andouille links, jambalaya heavy with rice, chicken, and seafood, gumbo filled with okra and it's dark roux base—I devoured them all. But my favorite was the Étoufée.

The roux—or mother sauce of flour mixed with fat drippings was used as a base for this, as well as for many other dishes. It was cooked on low to retain just the right consistency. The roux was stirred constantly to remove the undesirable flavor of the flour and bring out a deeper, nuttier character. This sauce could be left a lighter, blonde color, or cooked even longer until it became a darker, brown color. The longer it was cooked, the more pronounced the nutty flavor became.

The lovely sauce was then further seasoned, stuffed with shellfish of the patron's choosing and served over white rice. I particularly loved the crawfish version, but shrimp Étoufée was also quite popular. I felt a special connection to this meal. Though the fare was Creole in nature, it was a dish that felt very French to me.

On one of these journeys throughout the city, I also became introduced to a man named Fabien. Fabien lived in Lafayette and was visiting New Orleans to experience Mardi Gras. Upon conversing with him further, I learned that he and his brother were from Toulouse and had come to America after both graduating from Les Compagnons du

Devoir in pastry and carpentry, respectively. In fact, Fabien was one of the first to leave France and accomplish big things in America! He was well known as a top pastry chef in Lafayette, and his bakery has been in existence for forty plus years. It is still in business today.

I made an immediate bond with Fabien, and I am proud to still call him friend. We have kept in touch down through the years, and I make it a point to visit Lafayette every time that Danielle and I head to New Orleans. Even though I did not complete my training with Les Compagnons du Devoir, due to my illness, Fabien has always treated me with respect. He insists on including me in the inner circle as a true Les Compagnons man.

My first time in New Orleans was an experience, to say the least. I discovered treasures nestled amidst the debauchery, *certainement*—food and friendship. But I was never more grateful to be able to walk through my own front door in Dallas and fall into the open arms of my loving wife and children.

CRAWFISH ETOUFFEE

Ingredients: { Serves 6-8 }

½ cup butter, cubed
2 tbsp. all-purpose flour
1 cup celery, chopped
1 cup green pepper, chopped
½ cup red onion, chopped
1 lbs. broth ——————— 1 Qt. water with crab shell and crawfish shell — fish head optional.
1 cup water
¼ cup fresh parsley, minced
1 tbsp. tomato paste
1 bay leaf
Pinch salt, pepper, cayenne pepper
2 lbs. fresh crawfish tail meat
½ lbs. fresh crab meat (or blue crab)
hot cooked rice

Directions:

1. In a large, heavy skillet, melt the butter then stir in the flour. Stir over low heat for about 20 minutes, until it becomes a caramel-colored paste.
2. Add the celery, pepper, and onions. Stir.
3. Add broth, water, parsley, tomato paste, bay leaf, salt, pepper, and cayenne pepper. Bring to a boil.
4. Reduce heat, cover, and simmer slowly for about 30 minutes, stirring ocassionally. Add crawfish and heat through.
5. Serve with rice.

No. 32
Cheeseburger in Paradise

After my family had lived for only three short months in Dallas, and even after my booboo in New Orleans, Paul still recognized my potential and appreciated my abilities. I was promoted and sent to Houston to manage pastry and food in the company's thriving *café*. My position within the company was secure.

But, back in France, we were accustomed to Danielle also working to allow us to make ends meet. We were nervous because we knew that we would not have the luxury of a home being provided for us in Houston. Even with my promotion, it was still going to be a struggle if Danielle could not also find a job. To our dismay, we learned that at this time in America, there were strict rules in place regarding work visas for females.

The male head of the household could obtain a work visa typically with few issues. However, the female of the household's visa was required to be stamped, "Not Valid to Work." We did not know how we would make it. As difficult a hurdle as this would be to overcome, however, we knew that we had to follow the law. We resigned ourselves to figure something out.

When Danielle went to pick up her card, something short of miraculous occurred. Somehow, her visa did not get stamped. It should have, but strangely, it did not. We were saved! Danielle would now have the ability to find a job—which she would, at a different gourmet French bakery in Houston.

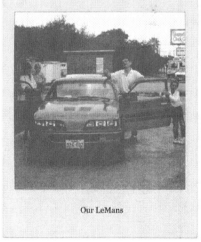

Our LeMans

A co-worker loaned me eight hundred dollars to buy a car. I chuckled when I settled on a Pontiac Le Mans. I must say, it was much different from the Le Mans that I was previously accustomed to. I was grateful, nonetheless, and we piled into the car with our few possessions. We drove the three and a half hours between Dallas and Houston with joy in our hearts. We were determined to carve out a home and a life for our family there.

And we did just that. We found a sweet little apartment that we were simply crazy over. We didn't have enough money saved right away to purchase furniture for our new apartment, but we were amazed to find out that we could rent furniture from a local company. Our apartment's balcony looked down over the community swimming pool. We often took pictures of our view to send back to our family in France. We had jobs, money for bills, a lovely, furnished home, food on the table, and each other. Who could ask for anything more?

With my promotion and Danielle's job, we relaxed our purse strings just a bit. We wanted a house of our very own, and the notion of owning my own bakery still tickled at the back of my mind. Nonetheless, we wanted to be able to experience the culture and food in our new homeland. The sheer size of the grocery stores astounded us. They were nothing like the markets that we were accustomed to. Suddenly, everything imaginable and then some, was available for purchase all under one roof. It still makes me laugh to remember how we found such joy in trying every single box of cereal that the cereal aisle had to offer. Every single one!

American cuisine was like nothing we had ever tasted before. We were dazed at the variety of choices all within close proximity and curious about them all. Pizza, Chinese, barbecue, hotdogs—we loved them all. What I had always longed to try, and what became my ultimate favorite American meal, was a thick, juicy burger, a side of fries, and a cold, refreshing Coke.

There was a particular place in Houston that served the best burgers. The sounds and the aroma of the fresh hamburger as it sizzled on the flat top made my heart skip a beat every time I walked through the door. Grease and juices from the seared meat ran down my hands. Gooey, melted cheese, fresh toppings, and just the perfect hint of condiments peeked out from atop the glorious patties. These were all crowned with the softest, freshest steamed bun in existence. Its consistency was nothing like any bread that I had made or eaten in France.

As if the burger wasn't delectable enough on its own, it was served with a side of mouthwatering French fries. When the hot, crisp, salty snap of the hand-cut sticks graced my tongue, I couldn't help but think that there was nothing French about these—they were purely American. The ice cold, bubbly sweet flavor of the cola was the perfect accompaniment and washed it all down. This food, this life—this was being an American! We absorbed every bit of the culture like sponges. We were truly in love with this country.

I will not fool you into thinking that life was a happily ever after fairytale. Our move to America—life in general— came with its ups and downs. The uprooting from all they had known and the transition into a new culture and life was tough for the kids. Aurore was just over two, so she did not notice it as much. But it was an especially difficult time for Franck. Imagine how it felt to a seven-year-old boy to be thrust into a whole new world and be forced to adapt. None of us knew the language except for Danielle. Our future path was still very much uncertain.

Despite the difficulties, we were making it work, and the important thing was that we were together. Life was good because we drew our strength from each other. Every day we learned, grew, and made our mark upon this country. And, we dreamed—above all, we dreamed. A house of our own and a bakery of our own—these were lofty goals, but not unattainable ones. Just being in America proved that. Our family—we were the American dream personified.

CHEESEBURGER + HAND·CUT FRIES

CHEESEBURGER:

Ingredients:

4 8oz. patties ground chuck
4 thick slices pepperjack
8 oz. cremini mushrooms, sliced & sauteed
8 slices thick-cut applewood bacon, cooked
8 slices tomato

4 slices red onions, thin
4 brioche buns
salt & pepper
unsalted butter

Directions:

Butter the buns while cooking meat. season the burgers with salt and pepper, then grill to your liking. Top each patty with mushrooms, bacon, and cheese while still on the grill. Wait until cheese melts.
Build the burgers using one patty per bun. Top with onions and tomatoes, and condiments of your choice.

FRIES:

Ingredients:

2 lbs. Idaho potatoes, cut into ½"-thick sticks
Peanut oil
salt & pepper

Directions:

Heat oil to 260°F in a large pot. Rinse the potatoes under cold water, then blanch them in the oil for 10 minutes. Remove from oil, and put them on a tray lined with paper towels. Raise heat on the oil to 350°F. Once the potatoes are completely cool, cook once more in the hot oil until golden brown and crisp. Remove from oil and place on fresh paper towels. season with salt and pepper.

Serve cheeseburgers with a side of fries.

Dreams Revisited

In a short time, the company that I worked for became a lovely, busy, popular, and flourishing business. When I was hired on in 1988, there were three *cafés* in existence. Flash forward to 1998, and there were seventy-two! With every year that I worked, I was given more responsibilities and duties. I was growing right along with the company.

Danielle went back to school to become certified as a travel agent in America. Soon after, she found a job. To say that our daily schedules were hectic would be quite the understatement. We still only owned one car, but we were creative and worked it all out.

Danielle dropped the kids off at school and daycare in the morning before she went to her job while I slept, as I worked the evening shift. In the afternoon, my friend Jacques and I would pick up the kids. Danielle and I would then pass like ships in the night. She would return home just long enough to hand me the car keys and kiss me goodbye. Then I would be off to work. Such was life every day. Trust me, it was not easy on our family or on our marriage. Knowing it was a necessity helped us to survive.

The thought of picking up the children every afternoon still makes me chuckle. Jacques drove a hideous old station wagon with wood paneling on the sides. Think of the car that you might recognize from those popular American movies. Now you understand, right?

Aurore attended a typical daycare, so there were no issues picking her up in such a monstrous car. But, thanks to a scholarship from the French consulate, Franck attended a very upscale private French school. Imagine Jacques and I pulling up in front of such a place to retrieve Franck after school. The dirty looks and disapproving stares from the other parents made us laugh out loud! Franck was mortified.

Danielle and I worked hard, pinched our pennies, and saved. As happy as I was in my position within the company, the thought of owning my own bakery still occasionally worked its way forward in my mind. Sometimes, on a whim, I checked on properties. Even despite our savings, everything was much too expensive. Rather, we moved forward with our second goal—buying a house. Three years after arriving in America, we rewarded ourselves and purchased a lovely little house in Houston.

We were shocked at how deluxe the house was. Plush wall-to-wall carpeting, walk-in closets, fancy bathrooms, and a fully equipped kitchen—the refrigerator even had an ice machine in the door! This house had it all. Over time, we even had our very own pool built in the backyard. We were literally living in a dream house.

Quite frankly, we were living in an all-around American dream. I was respected and well paid by my company, Danielle worked at a job that she loved, and the kids were accustomed to American life. We were the proud owners of a beautiful home. And every summer, my company paid for us to travel back to France to visit our families. Life was good.

But, in 1998, my boss Paul left the company, and it was sold to corporate investors. After Paul's departure, and because of the sale, the work environment completely changed. My job was no longer joyful, and I knew I needed a change. I gave my notice, and was determined to finally make my original goal of owning my own bakery in America come true. I contacted a Swiss-French man—let's call him Mathieu, whose bakery was for sale. I absolutely loved the property. Mathieu wanted an immediate fifty thousand dollars cash down to hold the bakery while we procured a bank loan for the rest. I was nervous. I did not have such wealth in my back pocket!

I was beginning to wonder if I had made the right decision in leaving my company. I had already given my notice, though, so ultimately I knew that there was nothing I could do. In the midst of my final days at the company, the new vice president approached me. I was both shocked and intrigued at what he proposed.

This man offered me a corporate chef position in Dallas. The new position would be even better than the one I was leaving, as I would be managing and supervising other chefs. The company even agreed to give my family twenty thousand dollars to help us relocate. A light bulb went off in my brain. Perhaps this was just the change that I was looking for. And perhaps, with time, I would be able to afford a bakery of my own after all. I heartily accepted the offer.

My family and I moved back to the Dallas area—to Plano—and I joyfully jumped right into my new position. As a corporate chef, I oversaw many talented people. They learned from me, and I learned from them, as well. One American chef in San Antonio particularly impressed me. This man offered a special pastry of the month in his *café,* and the customers went crazy over the idea. The month that I visited, he offered a scrumptious creation that blew my mind.

A moist, vanilla pound cake formed the base of the dessert. Sweet slices of canned peaches were layered atop the dense cake. Then on top of the peaches, he spooned a creamy cheesecake mixture. I was a bit skeptical at first— especially of the canned peaches. All doubts vanished when I tasted my first bite. The juice from the peaches permeated the top layer of the pound cake, which made the cake even moister. The sweetness of these two layers counterbalanced with the creamy tang of the cheesecake. All in all, it was a lovely dish.

In my new position, even meeting and shaping the practices of new people, having the chance to appreciate new ideas, and opening my mind to new techniques did not completely satisfy me. My mind continually wandered back to the bakery in Houston. It seemed just out of my reach, but that fact made me desire it all the more. The notion of fulfilling my dream lingered in my mind the way a fine wine lingers on the palate.

After eight long months as a corporate chef, my dissatisfaction with my position became more than I could bear. I did not want to merely supervise other bakers and chefs—I wanted to create! I wanted to feel the soft flour and the sticky dough on my hands again. I wanted to apply the knowledge that I had gained, both from recently and from across my span of years. I wanted to fashion mouth-watering fare that inspired others, as well as myself. I wanted to fill patrons' stomachs and hearts, and at the same time feed my own soul.

After we had moved to Plano, my family and I continued to live frugally and save as much as we could. Also, we had not touched the relocation money that my company had provided, and we even cleared a bit from the sale of our home in Houston. When I found out that Mathieu's bakery had not sold yet, it was as if all of the stars had aligned just for me. In 1998, I quit my corporate position and was financially able to make an offer on Mathieu's bakery.

Mathieu happily accepted the offer. He recognized my drive and passion and was as joyful to pass on his shop to me as I was to receive it. All that was left was to obtain a bank loan to fund the remaining $120,000 balance of the purchase price. We filled out the paperwork, and the waiting game began. My dream was so close now that I could almost reach out my fingertips and actually touch it.

How elusive dreams can be, sometimes. We made it all the way to the closing date when the bank informed us that they would not loan us the money after all. We were devastated. As close as my goal had been only days before, now it appeared to be impossible to reach.

Just as all seemed to be completely lost, Mathieu made a proposition that caused my heart to skip a beat. He agreed to owner finance the bakery on one condition: that if I was late in paying or missed a single payment, he would instantly reclaim the property. I humbly accepted his offer and vowed to honor it. I worked hard—never forgetting his generosity. Over the course of three years, I paid Mathieu back in full.

Once again, I had become master of my own destiny. As I woke each morning, this thought fueled my joy!

❧ poundcake cheesecake ❧

poundcake:
ingredients:
1 lbs. butter

1 lbs. sugar

.3 lbs. cake flour

.5 lbs. all-purpose flour

½ tsp. baking soda

.75 lbs. eggs

1 tsp. vanilla

½ lbs. sour cream

directions:
Mix the butter and sugar. Add the flour, then the rest of
the dry ingredients, gradually. Add the eggs and vanilla
gradually. Add the sour cream. Set aside.

cheesecake:
ingredients:
1.5 lbs. cream cheese

½ cup sugar

2 tbsp. lemon juice

1 tsp. vanilla

2 tbsp. sour cream

3 eggs

½ tsp. salt

directions:
Mix the cream cheese and sugar until smooth. Add the
lemon juice, vanilla, and sour cream. Gradually mix in the eggs,
and salt.

assembly:
Grease a 6" cake pan. Add ½ pound of the poundcake
batter. Layer in any sliced fruit of your choice, then add
½ pound of the cheesecake batter. Bake at 340° F for
35-40 minutes, until lightly golden brown. Let cool entirely
before removing from pan.

My Son, the Apprentice

Me, Mom and Franck

Every day, even in the midst of the stress of starting up a new business, I awoke with a smile on my face. This was what I was meant to do. As grateful as I was for my former company's generosity, running my own *café* brought out *la joie dans ma vie*—the joy in my life. I was soon to learn of my dear son's absence of joy, though. Finding meaning for his life would lead my son down an all too familiar path from my own youth.

Franck had taken a job as a waiter in our *café* the summer before his senior year of high school. As he had no car, we rode back home from work together. On these trips, we chatted about the shop, the day-to-day routine, and just life in general. It was a wonderful summer for me because I was able to bond even more with my son. About a month in, one conversation in particular absolutely floored me.

Before we begin, you must know, Franck was the type of guy to pour himself into something that he loved. He had learned the principle of hard work from his mother and me, he made good grades, and he was to be the first Tellier man to graduate from high school. I envisioned a university diploma in his future, as well, in something like engineering, as he enjoyed math and physics, or international studies, as he spoke three languages. So, imagine my surprise when I discovered that high school had become just another chore. He felt it was a complete waste of his time, and he did not want to go back.

As Franck opened up to me and shared his struggles, I became overwhelmed, myself. He had a lack of interest in general education, difficulties and lack of confidence, and was concerned at the thought of paying for university classes mostly on his own. I had no idea that his current path brought him no potential for joy. By then I had been around long enough to know that merely surviving was certainly not living. I asked if he wished to go into some sort of a trade. I had hopes that he would at least finish high school first, but perhaps this new suggestion would lead him down a happier path.

He seemed to warm to the idea and suggested cooking. Typical teenager—he was not at all interested in the thought of starting his day before dawn to work with pastry. I agreed to a trial run at our *café*. Franck worked hard, as I knew that he would, except I could tell that cooking did not captivate his soul.

I also noticed him peeking over his shoulder to spy upon the pastry side of our business. He told me one day that pastry appeared to be the "work of tenderness, attention, and finesse." He described my trade even better than I could have. When he asked to give it a try, of course I said yes.

In July, three days before his seventeenth birthday, Franck woke with me at three a.m. for his first day. I recognized passion and dedication in him from the very start. I expected that he would train for the rest of the summer, finish out his senior year, and return the following summer into a full-time apprenticeship. I was quite surprised when, three days after his senior year began, he asked if he could quit school and finish his apprenticeship immediately.

I would be lying if I told you that his interest did not bring me a great sense of pride. I was thrilled that he had found his calling in a trade that I treasured. But, I told him, "I think we'd better talk to your mother first." Later that evening, we ran the idea by Danielle. At first, she said, "Absolutely not!" She was afraid that he would be wasting his brain. Franck managed to convince her, though, and the next day he withdrew from school.

The very first day of Franck's official apprenticeship, I drew all of the kitchen staff together and presented him to them. I told them, "This is my son, Franck. He will be learning to become a pastry chef. I will be harder on him than I will be on any one of you. Please do not interfere, as this is the way. Thank you." Years later, Franck shared with me that he had nearly passed out from nerves after that announcement! But, he took his position seriously, listened to my instruction, and was a quick study.

Our days off were technically Sundays and Mondays, but I would bring Franck in with me on Mondays to prepare for the rest of the week. At first we tackled this prep work together. As he became more knowledgeable and experienced, I allowed him to take the lead. I would catch up on paperwork instead of having to take care of such drudgery during time that could be spent with my family.

Franck was responsible for making French *macarons*, coconut macaroons, ladyfingers, and *crème caramel*. His favorite delicacy of all was the milk chocolate covered pecan cookies. I can understand why. These treats were simple, yet oh so delicious. The crisp, buttery cookie was heavenly enough. Add in toasted, chopped pecans and the cookie was taken to a whole new level due to their rich, deep flavor. Cover this with a layer of sweet, decadent milk chocolate, and the indulgence was sent over the top.

With proper instruction and time, Franck excelled at the craft. He became my right hand man, and it felt good having him by my side. The first Christmas Eve of his training, in between two immensely busy days, we napped on the flour sacks in the back room. This hearkened back bygone days and memories for me. And when we constructed elaborate pranks together, it was just like I was a teenager again working at my own apprenticeship with Damien.

One prank I will especially never forget, and I'm sure that neither will he. Franck crawled into a broken down bench fridge in the kitchen and I "went to work" at finding a victim to potentially scare. It was difficult, because finding a good reason to get one of the wait staff to come into the kitchen to get some milk from this fridge was out of the ordinary. You see, even though this fridge was broken, it was used by the kitchen staff as a workbench. Only the wait staff did not know it was out of order, so we had to find our victim from the front of house. The first two employees grabbed the milk from a closer station and handed it to me. Not wanting to blow the joke, I simply smiled and thanked them.

I'm sure that Franck was starting to sweat inside that claustrophobic, smelly fridge. But he was like a soldier. Finally, an employee agreed to get the milk and opened the door. Franck was ready. He reached out and grabbed our victim with all his might. I have never heard a man scream so high to this day! The whole kitchen was in tears.

Jokes like these went on and on. All we needed were simple things like burlap sacks from a delivery of vegetables, and plans began to brew. We especially loved to joke when the workload was heavy and the mood and morale tended to drop. Sometimes, we even crafted pranks on our way in to work. It was a way for me to lighten the stress, relive my youth, and make memories with my son— all at the same time

Franck's apprenticeship was a journey down memory lane for me. It was also a journey of discovery for the both of us. We both had to recognize the difference between the father/son dynamic and the boss/mentor one. Discovery such as this is not an easy task, but I think that Franck put it best when he said, "We were both having an apprenticeship—one of a boy learning his father's trade, and one of a father learning to be with his son through the trade he loves."

pecan cookies

ingredients:

20
~~8~~ oz. cold butter, cubed
8 oz. sugar
4 oz. brown sugar
20 oz. cake flour
12 oz. finely ground pecan
12 oz. pecan pieces

1 tsp. vanilla paste
1 pinch lemon zest
½ tsp. salt
4 oz. egg whites
milk chocolate, for garnish

directions:

1. Combine sugar, brown sugar, flour, all pecans, and salt. Add the butter and mix with a paddle until it reaches a sandy consistency. Add the egg whites, vanilla paste, and lemon zest, stirring until it becomes a dough.

2. Roll out the dough to create a heart (or a bunch of small hearts). Bake on a cookie sheet at 320 °F for 20 minutes or until golden brown. Let cool.

3. Using a spoon, drizzle melted chocolate across the cookies. Serve while still warm.

No. 35
Tragedy and Patriotism

Once Franck started asking too many technical questions, I decided that he needed a more in depth education. Danielle and I both agreed it was the best for him. We found a school in Rouen, France—the Institut National de la Boulangerie Pâtisserie. After two years of apprenticeship with me, Franck was ready to attain his French pastry and *boulangerie* diplomas. I saw this as a way for him to fine-tune his apprenticeship. He knew how to do so much, but he still did not quite know why he was doing it. The INBP could open that door for him.

Before Franck departed for France, his former high school's principal insisted that he obtain his GED. The fact that an honor roll student dropped out of high school had never sat well with her. She simply would not take no for an answer, so Franck complied with her request. Danielle and I were both extremely proud at the man that he had become. He was educated in both the American way, as well as in the school of life. And soon, he would be educated in the French way.

Franck studied in Rouen for a year. After achieving his diplomas, he worked post-graduation at a hotel restaurant in Ensisheim, Alsace, or the German influenced part of France. Meanwhile, back in Houston, our first bakery/*café* continued to be quite successful. Our shop was nominated for the best pastry shop in Houston and would receive this honor a total of six different times while under our care. We were also sharing beautiful French dishes with our local community. Our customers adored such fare.

Our spirits fell along with the twin towers on September 11, 2001. The horror of it all! We did not know what to think. In all my life, the closest that I had come to knowing such savagery was when I listened to my grandfather talk about his prisoner of war days. We expressed our compassion to those in our community, and grieved along with the nation. In late 2001 to mid 2002, America began to slowly pick up the pieces. Grief and outrage were still present, but life began to work its way back toward what it was before the tragedy had rocked everyone's foundations.

Our business was steady and, in fact, began to boom. We could finally take a breath, quit pinching our pennies so tightly, and even go on vacation that summer. I felt energized because of this and aspired to open yet a second bakery. The property was purchased, preparations were made, and we happily opened our doors on the 1st of September 2002.

But shortly afterward, when France's president refused to support President Bush's policy regarding Iraq, my family—as well as those of other French nationals—was unfortunately placed in a very tough position. We were still patriotic to France, of course. It was our home country. Still, we felt such love and sympathy for America, as well as an affinity toward our local community and its people. It was a very thin line to walk across.

To make matters worse, workers began to strike and certain customers refused to frequent our bakeries because of our heritage. One day, a certain customer inquired as to Danielle's accent. When he found out she was French, he swore he would not come back to our establishment. Many locals knew us well, and still supported us. In fact, another customer in line defended Danielle and our family's honor.

We tried our best to share our views and our position with both the rest of our staff and the community members who did not know us so well. Even so, this did not always work. Times became difficult. The prosperity that we had known such a short while before was once again elusive and fleeting.

As they always do, the difficulties passed. Eventually the tempers that had flared so brightly settled down once more, the community came to realize that we were not the problem, and the people came back. When Franck returned home, fully trained, he helped us to turn things around. His work ethic, charm, and an infusion of his younger blood and mindset were exactly what our shops needed.

I'm not saying that it was easy. It took a while to completely regain the trust of a few patrons in our area. We had staff issues to be dealt with—particularly the management of our second bakery. And it took a bit of time

143

for Franck and I to come to a full understanding of each other and our roles. I needed to trust in his abilities enough to allow him to be more than my former apprentice, and he needed to learn that I was not finished teaching him, either.

Upon returning home, Franck told me that during his

time in Rouen he was eager to absorb as much as he could. His express purpose was to come back to our family business and continue to build what we had begun. My heart swelled with pride. It did not take long before we were working together like a hand and a glove. Our shops began to flourish.

Franck came back to America with a head full of knowledge and the desire to share it, *certainement!* He was especially proud of the *kouglof* recipe that he had picked up while working in Alsace. It was delicious! The lightly sweet brioche coffee cake studded with golden raisins became an instant favorite—to most of our customers, that is.

One day, a lady came into the bakery and was shocked that our case was stocked with *kouglof*. She was of Alsatian descent, and happy to purchase a delicacy that originated from her area. The next day, she came back to the shop. We smiled as we inquired if she was back for more *kouglof*. Our smiles soon turned to frowns. Her answer was a disinterested no. She claimed that our version of the sweet treat was too dry, but she offered a "better" recipe to us— her own grandmother's. We accepted the recipe, but scoffed after she had gone about her way. Her recipe was nothing like Franck's.

Even so, our interest was piqued. We made a batch of her version of the *kouglof,* thinking that we would call her bluff. Truth was that we were the ones who were proven wrong! Her recipe was light, airy, and its moist consistency made our first version seem more like paper than pastry. I guess even we still had room to learn. Believe me, it was quite a delicious lesson.

kouglof

Ingredients:

5 oz. eggs   1 Pinch salt

5 oz. milk   2 oz. golden Raisins, marinated in Rum
                                     for 24 hours

~~striked out~~   8 oz. soft butter

1/4 tsp. dry Yeast   3 oz. sugar

1 lbs. flour

Directions:

1. Mix flour, Yeast, sugar, salt, milk, and eggs. Use the second speed on the mixer with a paddle for 8 minutes.
2. Add Raisins and butter. Let sit for 1 hour. cover with wet towels, then
3. Flatten the dough and put into a kouglof mold. ↑ Let Proof for 6-8 hours, OR until dough has doubled in size.
4. Bake at 340°F for 35-38 minutes. Remove from Oven and let Rest 4-5 minutes. Flip it out of the pan.
5. Optional: mix 1/2 cup butter, 1/2 cup sugar, and 1/2 cup Rum, and Pour on top.

No. 36
Say Cheese!

Life went well for us for years after we turned our fortune—and our bakeries—back around. There were the typical ups and downs, but such is the way, is it not? We all worked to build our businesses, Franck met and later married his lovely wife, Liz, and we prepared to expand our business, once again. Life was certainly good. But, have you noticed that in the midst of blue skies, storm clouds still have a habit of brewing?

After our second bakery was up and on its way, our landlord decided to raise the rent on the property an exorbitant amount—by $5,000.00 per month. It was completely uncalled for. I will never understand human nature regarding money. To me, greed is an unnecessary evil. On top of this, Danielle's right hand woman, who was in charge of our first bakery, was not fulfilling her role in the manner that we saw fit.

In the midst of all of this, Franck and Liz came to us with news. They were weighing the pros and cons of accepting her company's offer of a new position. It would require them to move to Australia. Danielle and I were surprised, as well as genuinely happy for such an opportunity to arise for them.

We could feel the winds of change blowing in our faces. I have noticed many different times over the years that life is very much like the wind—always changing direction. We must all learn to adapt to those changes—to go the way the wind takes us. Rather than fight with the greedy landlord, Danielle and I chose to sell our bakeries. It was a tough decision, but we felt it to be a good one. The real estate market in Houston was exploding at that time, so our properties sold rather quickly, and we came away with a decent profit. There were still some loose ends to tie up, though.

One of the terms of the sale was for me to stick around to continue working and managing until the new owner was sufficiently trained. I worked for eight long months at this—with Franck by my side the whole time. He and his wife placed their plans on hold to help Danielle and me. Finally, we were able to break free from this arrangement. Meanwhile, Franck and Liz were having doubts about the practicality of their potential move. But what is practical about truly living? Some of our best moments come from taking a scary, impossible leap into the unknown.

We gave Franck and Liz this advice and our blessing—to not resist life's changing wind, but to allow it to push them in a new direction. And we took the same advice, ourselves. Danielle and I weren't sent in an unfamiliar direction, but rather, a very familiar one. Remember when I told you that I would never move back to France? I was about to be forced to eat my words. My mother had taken ill, and rather than bring her to America with us, we decided to go to France to be with her.

Our plan was to move full-time into the vacation house that we already owned. It was situated rather close to Danielle's parents. We'd move Mother in with us, buy a bakery nearby, and live happily—all in that order. Half of our plan came to pass right away. Our sweet little house in the Pyrenees wasn't as modern as our Houston home, but we loved it, nonetheless. And we were indeed happy.

We shared in more than a few delightful experiences back in our home country. One of these in particular was rediscovering the covered market in Danielle's village. Who would've guessed that the very same cheese vendor whose wares we had savored many years before was still set up there? We were ecstatic!

A chef friend from America who had never visited France before came to call, and we could not wait to share these delicious cheese samplings with him. The vendor had a little shop nearby and invited us all for a tour. Danielle and I were thrilled during the tour because we appreciated the effort this man put into his craft as he manipulated and molded the cheese with his bare hands. Remember, I told you it was the best cheese in the world.

Our friend wrinkled his nose at the sight. A hairy-armed man with those arms almost elbow-deep in cheese—and wearing no gloves, at that. Our friend was astonished. Ahh, but he changed his mind when he was given the first sample taste. When the soft, creamy cheese touched his tongue, the flavor alone won our friend over.

The cheese vendor's eyes twinkled as he told us he had a surprise to show us. We walked to the back of his shop. He fished a set of keys out of his pocket, unlocked a heavy door, and pushed it open. Our mouths instantly began to water. Rows upon rows and shelves upon shelves of glorious rounds of cheese awaited us in this room. The vendor explained that this was, in fact, the good stuff.

You see, the government had certain regulations in place regarding cheese making. Each round of cheese was to be housed and aged in wooden casings for sanitation purposes. This storage method slightly compromised the flavor of the cheese, in his opinion. The best cheese was that which was allowed to breathe. The vendor complied with the health department's demands, as any responsible shopkeeper would. Still, he felt that he owed it to his craft to create as it originally was done, and as it should be done.

Cheese making for him was not a business—it was a labor of love and an art form. Very few people were allowed to view his secret room, as the government did not know about it. We felt very honored that we were included among the chosen few. When our tour was completed, we purchased some of the delicious cheese, passed along our sincere thanks, and went about our way. After we left his shop, we all laughed as we noticed that our clothing was perfumed with the scent of cheese.

A plan had already formed in my mind for how I was going to prepare the delicacy that I had procured. At home, I set to work. I peeled slightly firm pears, delicately sliced them, and pan fried them in butter. I then caramelized these golden slices with sweet, local honey. I cut samplings of the creamy, decadent sheep's milk cheese into sticks that were then wrapped with thin slices of salty Pyrenean ham. These cloaked sticks were then shrouded in the delectable pear slices.

The sticks were finally pierced with tooth picks to hold the delicious layers together and then finished off with a gentle sprinkle of freshly ground black pepper. They were a creamy, salty, sweet masterpiece. A crisp bottle of local wine complemented the snack perfectly—this was as close to heaven as a menu could get!

It was a joy finding this man still in business after so many years. After all, Danielle had purchased cheese from this very vendor at the tender age of fifteen. His two daughters plan to take over the running of the family business when the gentleman retires. Their dedication to preserving their father's craft was inspirational. It is my hope that this same shop will survive and that my children's children will visit the area and prize such decadent cheese.

Yes, Danielle and I were happy in France. Although, I have found that happiness is a fickle friend—present one minute, and gone the next. We came to discover that my mother was not merely ill. She suffered from a combination of both Alzheimer's and dementia. Sadly, we would not be able to minister to her needs as we had originally hoped. She would require much more intensive care than we could provide. We arranged for such care because what mattered the most was her well-being.

Meanwhile, we moved forward in search of a bakery. This quest proved to be more daunting than we imagined. We hoped to discover the perfect storefront in Paris. We had loved living there years previously, and we felt if we planned to stay in the country, then the sort of culture we were looking for could be found there. We made an offer on a bakery, but it was rejected.

We were surprised to find that, even in Paris, the mentality of running a bakery was still very much old fashioned in nature. It was the same old style bakery model that had existed all of my life—the one that we had moved away from in the nineteen eighties. Properties were too expensive to be profitable, and there was no safety or proper governmental regulations in place for the workers. There had been no progressive thinking, no modernization—no change. At that time, *café*-style bakeries like those we had prospered from in America were not in existence.

We ran into disappointment in every region and around every turn. It was all the same story. After a similar visit to Toulouse, when a shop owner asked an exorbitant amount for his property and would not even share his numbers so we could figure out some semblance of profit margins, our disenchantment showed on our faces. That evening, Danielle and I looked at each other and simultaneously spoke the words that had lodged themselves both on our hearts and in our heads. "We must go back to America."

The American dream called to us again. And just like before, we answered that call. Would we rediscover all that we once had known?

Pyrenean Pur Brebis Bouchées

ingredients:

2 pears (firm)
8 oz. Pyrenean Sheep cheese
8 Pyrenean ham slices, very thin
1 oz. butter
1 tsp. honey

directions:

1. Peel the pears, and slice them very thin.
2. Put butter in a hot fry pan, and cook until golden, about 2 minutes.
3. Cut the Pyrenean cheese into medium size sticks, wrap them with the ham, and with the caramelized pear slices.
4. Stick each with a toothpick to hold together.
5. Sprinkle with fresh pepper.

No. 37
Hokie Hi: Tech Triumph

Danielle and I arrived in America for the second time not quite under the same circumstances as we did the first time, but there was one definite parallel. Once again, I desired to own my own bakery. We returned to Houston to the open arms of Franck, Liz, and Aurore. We found hospitality and shelter in Liz and Franck's home, but they were finally tying up loose ends of their own and preparing to move to Australia. We did not wish to hold them back. Immediately we set to work.

We searched nationwide for bakeries that were on the market. We were determined. We followed up on leads and visited all corners of the country—Texas, Maine, Seattle, Boston, and Denver—we searched them all. Just like our experiences in France, we kept running into dead ends. If a property was viable, it was much too expensive for profitability. Or, if financial practicality was in order, the property itself did not suit our needs.

A random telephone call to a Virginia-based friend near the Washington, D.C. area provided us with one more lead. He asked us if we had ever heard of Blacksburg, Virginia, because he knew that a well-established bakery had been placed on the market there. We decided to pay the area a visit. We were hopeful, but anxious at the same time. Danielle and I had run into so many disappointments. We did not want this lead to be yet another.

We visited in September of 2008. The autumn leaves were not dressed in their finery just yet, but we could feel the crispness in the air. The mountains were not nearly as tall as the Pyrenees, or snow-capped, but otherwise the terrain and the oncoming season was quite similar to that of our homeland. The town was quaint and homey, and it was obvious that the local university, Virginia Tech, fueled the heart of the town. We were pleased with the area. Would we be as pleased with the bakery?

It was just as my friend had described; the bakery was indeed well established. The bakery's owner, Lauren, was a kind woman who had been devoted to the running of her shop for twenty-nine years. Danielle and I saw the bakery's potential straightaway. We returned to our hotel later that evening and discussed whether or not there was potential for a future for us in the area. We felt certain that there was. Hope soared within the both of us, and we planned to make Lauren an offer.

This would not turn out to be an easy task. You see, before we had left for France, we invested a large portion of our profits from the sale of all of our properties in the hopes that the money would see growth. The stock market crash hit us rather hard. Yet again, we were financially in an uncomfortable state of affairs. We did not know how we would come up with the necessary funding to follow through on our offer for the bakery, but we were undaunted in the task. Somehow we would find a way.

At first we could not come to an agreement with Lauren. We went back to our search in the interim, but to no avail. It took six months and a return visit to the area before a deal was firmly established. Our resolve paid off, though, and the funding came through—just as we hoped that it would. Danielle and I moved to Blacksburg on April 1, 2009. We opened the bakery under our care and management on April the 17th—just one day after the second anniversary of the April 16th tragedy at Virginia Tech.

I was happy to have discovered a bakery that was such an integral part of the vibrant surrounding community. We added our French flair to an already beautiful and purposeful business. To honor the former owner and her years of dedication, we kept some of her former recipes on our menu. Her chicken salad was savory with its vinegar base, and the sweet crunch of cranberries was a surprise to the palate. Her scones were delightful, with just the right density, although where she mixed the fruit within the dough, I placed it on top for show. And her strudel recipe was a sweet, tempting addition to my repertoire.

However, I brought quite the dish to Blacksburg's table, myself. Back in Houston, our customers had fallen in love with my Chicken in Riesling recipe. The dish was lovely. A fresh, whole chicken was cut into pieces and sautéed. It was then marinated in a smooth Riesling wine for twenty-four hours. After marinating, the chicken and the wine were both placed in a pan along with pork belly, mushrooms, onions, and bay leaves. This mixture was cooked slowly on a low heat. The sauce was reduced, and cooled. Then velvety sour cream was added, as well as fresh parsley, for brightness. The soft dumpling-like egg noodle, *spaetzle*, was the perfect accompaniment for such a richly flavored chicken.

My new customers were just as enamored with this fare as my old ones had been. Blacksburg, Virginia, had been introduced to a French delicacy by way of Houston, Texas. What a wonderful dish! And what a wonderful world!

Chicken and Riesling

serves 4

ingredients:

4 shallots

whole chicken (2-2.5 lbs), cut in 4

4 cloves garlic

2 bay leaves

1 cup sour cream

2 stalks celery

8 slices bacon

1 bottle Riesling wine

2 lbs. white mushrooms, quartered

1 bunch fresh thyme

salt, pepper, nutmeg

pinch coriander

butter, as needed

directions:

1. Cut chicken in 4. Marinate chicken in the Riesling with the bay leaves for at least 4-6 hours. Do not throw out the marinade.

2. Dice the bacon very thin, and sautee it with the chicken in butter until golden brown.

3. Add the shallots, garlic, and celery. Cover with the wine marinade, mushrooms, and thyme. Simmer for 45 minutes to 1 hour.

4. Remove everything from the pan except the liquid and transfer to a serving dish. Add the sour cream until melted, then pour the liquid over the chicken. Serve.

No. 38
Give Us This Day Our Daily Bread

In Blacksburg, Virginia, and the New River Valley, Danielle and I found a cozy, beautiful community nestled amongst the mountains. And believe me, I am not just referring to the seasons or the scenery. The people were so warm and friendly. Danielle and I had never felt so welcomed anywhere else in the world, short of our own villages. This was very encouraging to us.

Within the locality, there was obvious dedication to the arts, to showcasing local goods and culture, and to the joy of food. We also appreciated that the area was so supportive of local start-ups. Very few chain restaurants were—or still are—in existence within Blacksburg's lively and popular downtown area. The eateries mostly had been started by individuals or families, much like Danielle and I had done. It was very refreshing.

We loved the local farmer's market. It reminded us of the one in Danielle's village, and we were happy to see people growing and harvesting from their land. We frequented the farmer's market on a regular basis and got to know many of the local vendors, as well as the townspeople that shared a similar love for the harvest to table movement.

Recognizing and forming relationships with these Virginians became common practice for Danielle and me. This was all relatively new to us. Of course we had our locals that habitually patronized our bakeries in Houston.

157

But the area was so large that it proved easy to fall into the big city mindset of keeping up with only your own life. Small town living is much, much different.

Yes, we were fostering relationships with the local people and we felt so beautifully welcomed to the area. But, I will admit, the early days of running the bakery were difficult ones. You will recall that Our Daily Bread had been well established within the community for twenty-nine years. When we took over, even though we preserved some of the former owner's recipes, the menu board looked quite different than what the people were accustomed to seeing.

Our offerings were decidedly French. The *croissants* and *baguettes*, pastry creations, and the meals all had our signature French flair. For some, this was a wonderful thing. We were shocked at how many people came to us and asked if we served certain French dishes. When we inquired as to how they knew about such particular fare, they excitedly spun tales of vacationing, wintering in France, or frequenting French restaurants in larger cities across the United States.

Luckily for us, many people love to embrace what is new and different. Not recognizing the name of a dish on a menu board, or not knowing that dish's ingredients poses no problem for such individuals. For others, spending their hard-earned money on trying a cuisine that they may or may not enjoy can cause speculation. I was a bit nervous, myself, when sampling certain American or Americanized food for the first time. Would such offerings prove satisfying? This was the question that formed in my mind, and I'm sure a similar question floated around in the minds of some of those within our new community.

As always, we did not let circumstances deter our drive or our work ethic. We worked hard, because it was all that we had ever done. It was all that we knew to do. I led the kitchen team, and Danielle took care of the business end, along with the front of the house.

Honestly, it took a while for business to boom, but once it did, oh, *mon dieu*—oh my, did it ever! I remember a time when Saturday hours used to crawl by. Suddenly, we were busy beyond anything we had seen. We did not know where the change came from, but we absolutely loved it.

Our customers took home loaves of bread to savor and praised our menu offerings. What especially warmed my heart is that they always saved room for our sweet treats—and they still do. They were enchanted with our dainty, sweet French *macarons*. Their eyes widened at the trays of multi-colored confections like a child's would when spying shelves of candy. They oohed and ahhed at our lovely handmade cakes. And they raved over our almond macaroons.

The sweet, almost cherry-like flavor of almond has always been a favorite of mine. Whipping the almond paste with egg whites and sugar caused the macaroon's batter to possess a light and airy quality. After being piped into a lovely shape, topped with granulated sugar, and popped into the oven, the whole kitchen would become fragranced with cloyingly sweet perfume.

Pulling these treats from the oven was a task anyone would volunteer for. Their crackled, crunchy exterior hid a soft, chewy interior. This tender interior was exposed only as the delicacy was pulled apart to be consumed. What flavor, what texture! It was worth the burnt fingertips to tear right into one of these luxuries straight from the oven.

With the endearment we felt toward the community and business steadily progressing, we felt that our future in this area could be as luminous as we had hoped it would be only one short year before. We bought and moved into our current home a year after we arrived in Blacksburg. As we tramped up and down our snowy driveway to retrieve our belongings from the moving truck, even the cold of mid-January could not chill the warmth of our hearts. We were home. Yes, we were home.

almond macaroons

ingredients:
1 lbs. almond paste
1/2 lbs. sugar
.3 lbo. egg whites

directions:

1. With a paddle mixer, combine almond paste and sugar until they reach a sandy consistency. Very gradually add the egg whites, still mixing, until a smooth paste is formed. Continue mixing on high speed for 2 minutes — it should become smoother and lighter in color.

2. Line a sheet tray with parchment paper. Using a piping bag with a star tip, pipe rosettes about 2 1/4" in diameter. Sprinkle with sugar.

3. Bake at 340° F for 18-22 minutes or until golden. Top with powdered sugar if desired.

No. 39
Generations

Our new bakery was busy and profitable. And roughly two years after the opening of Our Daily Bread, it was considered to be well established enough by Les Compagnons du Devoir standards for me to begin to receive apprentices. To make this point clear, if you had trained at Les Compagnons and the institution deemed both you and your business worthy and credible, a working relationship would be set into motion. Accordingly, the school began to send us apprentices, as they did to all of the other deserved bakeries. The institution's association with me has been longstanding. They still continue to send me apprentices to this day.

These apprentices are granted special work visas and are allowed to remain in the country for one year. Though they are Les Compagnons graduates already and quite skilled, in this year they receive even more practical training and a paycheck to go along with it. Thankfully for them, their earnings do not match mine from my first apprenticeship! Back in 1973, I received a wage of the approximation of twenty U.S. dollars a month. My, how times have changed!

The year these apprentices spend in America is a very useful time period, both for the apprentices and for the host bakery. The apprentices learn the nature of business, further work ethic, American culture, and development. And the host gets to reap the rewards of top-notch, skilled labor. It is a win-win situation for all involved.

One particular apprentice of mine did not come to me from Les Compagnons. No, I discovered this apprentice under very special circumstances. You see, down through the years, I had remained friends with my former boss, Monsieur Pelotte. We spoke quite frequently on the phone, and I cherished his mentorship as well as his friendship. In the process, I was introduced to the Monsieur's nephew, Eduard. Eduard frequently joined our phone conversations, and soon became a trusted friend of mine, as well. He was always quite interested in where I was located and what I was doing.

Eduard received his training from his uncle, just as I had done many years before. To hear about his work life struck me with nostalgia because it closely paralleled my own from once upon a time. With his uncle's training under his belt, Eduard grew into a fine chef in his own right. Appropriately, at a young age, he acquired a bakery of his own, and managed it with skill and finesse.

One day, a few short years ago, I received what I thought was a typical phone call from Eduard. After our opening pleasantries, Eduard informed me that he had a particularly skilled apprentice of almost twenty years of age who wished to come to America. He inquired if I would be willing to take the young man, Lorenzo, under my wing. Lorenzo was of French and Italian descent and was highly recommended by Eduard. I trusted Eduard's judgment fully, so how could I say no?

Imagine, so many years after I had originally worked for Monsieur Pelotte, I would befriend his nephew, Eduard, who would train under the Monsieur just as I once had. Eduard now prepared to send me an apprentice who had trained under him, and would complete his training under my supervision. It all started in Paris and would carry on halfway across the globe in Blacksburg, Virginia. Four generations of men all with similar training and similar purpose—to learn, to work hard, and to share a love of pastry. It was indeed a small world.

162

Lorenzo was beyond excited to be in America. He loved everything about the country—the culture, the scenery, and the food. His reactions reminded me of my own first experiences in the United States. Lorenzo brought with him a wealth of training, as well as recipes from his region, the French Riviera. One certain recipe hearkened to both his French and Italian roots.

Pain de Gênes is a lovely cake that was created by the Italians. After its conception, the Italian *amour* with the sweet treat fell by the wayside, but the French carried on its design. This melt-in-your-mouth cake came from Genoa, thus its name. The best almond paste can be found in this area, and this, along with a fair amount of butter and sugar, flavors the cake.

To make this cake truly authentic, a special parchment-style paper that is stamped Pain de Gênes is placed on the bottom of the pan before the batter is poured on top and the dessert is baked. Without the paper, the cake it just a replica of the actual dessert. Adding the paper is traditional and makes the pastry bona fide. What a delicate confection. Why the Italians stopped making it, I will never know. But their loss is France's gain.

Even now, Lorenzo is still in my employ, but he is no longer just my apprentice. He now serves as my chef de cuisine. Since the day that he arrived in America, I have been grateful for his talent. His work ethic, dedication, and love of pastry match my own zeal when I was his age. I look forward to creating many more beautiful masterpieces with him in the future. When I speak to Eduard on the telephone—which, yes, I still do—now he not only inquires about me, but about Lorenzo, as well. Four generations— one small world.

PAIN DE GÊNES

ingredients:

1 lbs almond paste	1 tsp. baking powder
.3 lbs powdered sugar	2 tbsp rum — martinique suggested
.9 lbs eggs	.4 lbs. butter, melted and at room ~~temperature~~ temperature
.3 lbs cake flour	

directions:

1. combine almond paste and powdered sugar and mix with a paddle until they reach a sandy consistency.
2. gradually add the eggs until the mixture reaches a ~~fla~~ fluffy, smooth texture. fold in the flour. once combined, fold in the butter, vanilla, and rum.
3. prepare three greased 9" pans, lined with parchment paper. pour batter evenly in the pans. bake at 375° F for 14 minutes.

Daddy's Not So Little Girl

I can liken bakery life over the past few years in Blacksburg, Virginia to what I have grown accustomed to over the course of my *la folie* forty—a life of work, joyfulness, and one blessed with new challenges and possibilities every single day. I am certainly not the young man that I once was, but my heart, drive, and love of cuisine are all still very much intact. Thankfully, I am surrounded by a capable staff whose determination, ability, and hearts all match and complement my own. I took on a whole new set of joys and challenges in February of 2014 by expanding further into the New River Valley. My Roanoke store has since become a lovely, accomplished sister property to my Blacksburg one.

A large part of my heart belongs to pastry, and to my businesses, *c'est vrai*—it is true. That portion is small in comparison to the part that belongs to my family. They are my world. I adore waking up every day and working side by side with my lovely wife. I am so proud of my son—for following in my footsteps, for following his heart, and for allowing the winds of change to send him in an adventurous direction. He is now a brand new father, and I know that my grandson, Logan, will someday be grateful to

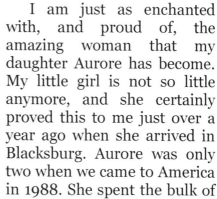

be able to call such a man Dad.

I am just as enchanted with, and proud of, the amazing woman that my daughter Aurore has become. My little girl is not so little anymore, and she certainly proved this to me just over a year ago when she arrived in Blacksburg. Aurore was only two when we came to America in 1988. She spent the bulk of her life in Houston and absolutely loved it there. But with my Roanoke expansion in the works, I wanted another capable Tellier to round out my staff and work by my side.

I invited Aurore to transition away from her life in Houston and make Virginia her home. Being the good daughter that she is, she answered my call with a resounding yes. I knew my request would ultimately be a huge change for her. She had only spent a few random long weekends in the area, and her life had always revolved around the familiar in Houston. Being a Tellier, I knew that the act of embracing change ran through her blood.

She, and her now *fiancé,* Gabriel, made the move to Blacksburg. The transition was equally great for him, because he, too, left all that he had known. I am beyond proud when I say that they both jumped right into the family business with enthusiasm, faith, and optimism. I can only hope that later in life when they look back on their own life stories, they will remember this period of change with fondness.

I do know one thing for certain—it warms my heart every day to work in the kitchen with my future son-in-law, a multi-faceted and talented executive chef. And it brings me such joy to watch my daughter so skillfully manage the demands of the front of the house. These two not only have a passion for each other, but a passion for food, and a passion for life. It is a beautiful thing.

Aurore's love of food comes naturally. Early in her school days, she watched me prepare dinner while she finished her homework at the kitchen table. Every afternoon I would either pick up the kids from school, or be home shortly after they got off the bus. Franck would immediately go to do homework or relax in his room. Not my Aurore. She wanted to be right in the middle of the action.

Sometimes, if she finished her work quickly enough, she would peel the carrots or help chop the potatoes for me. An hour later, and *voila!* The kitchen was filled with the delicious aroma of a simple home-cooked meal. We were not a family that ate fast food every day as we struggled to balance schedules or went out to restaurants on a weekly basis. Nor did we have a fridge full of sodas or a pantry full of unhealthy snacks. This was not our way. We always ate healthy meals, and no matter how busy our individual schedules were, every evening we ate dinner together. Always.

Isn't it amazing how such a simple daily routine could instill in a young person such a deep love and respect for food? Simple acts, done with great love, can certainly change the world. It thrills me that Aurore now knows how to cook because of me. She treats cuisine with love, imagination, and confidence.

Similar to when I cook at home, she rarely follows a recipe. I have learned over the years to recognize how flavors will meld and how ingredients will taste together in my mind, and she has done the same. She claims that she doesn't always know what will come out of her dishes, but that she knows to trust herself enough to make something that will warm her soul. Truly, that is what cuisine is all about.

Aurore is a genius in the kitchen when it comes to making chili. As you know, she was born in Martinique, but she lived the majority of her life in Texas. She calls herself a proud French-Texan, and, according to her, every good Texan knows a good chili. It took years for Aurore to perfect her chili recipe, or so she tells me. And while this isn't a typical dish that I serve, I will admit that a piping hot bowl of it on a cold autumn evening is very satisfying.

The rich tomato base is accentuated by the perfect amount of seasoning. Too much, and the flavor becomes overbearing, not enough and it is weak. There has to be just the right balance. The hearty consistency and punch of spice in this dish warms a person from head to toe. And the tequila added into the mix doesn't hurt, either! It is fare that truly represents the warm vibrancy of the southwest.

There weren't many cold evenings to speak of in Houston. Aurore used to settle for just a tiny chill in the air to use as an excuse to make a large pot of her chili. But, here in Virginia, as late summer leads into early fall, we can feel the change in the air coming on. When the leaves begin to color the mountainsides and the air is filled with cool crispness, there's no better time to dust this recipe off.

Aurore isn't a pony-tailed little girl chopping carrots

after homework anymore. She is a professional young woman, and Danielle and I recognize this more and more every day. Not every family has the chance to work together, to learn from each other, or to experience relationship dynamics on so many different levels. Not every family even wants such opportunities. I am—we are—so very grateful for every single one.

FRENCH TEXAN'S CHILI

ingredients:

2 lbs. ground buffalo
4 strips thick bacon, diced
2 cans "Red Gold" Petite Diced tomatoes
     w/ chipotle

1 can kidney beans
2 cans black beans
4 large tomatoes, chopped
5 celery stalks, chopped
1 ½ Red onions, chopped
garlic, to taste
1 green or Red bell pepper

2 beers - Preferably
       corona

1 or 2 shots tequila
7 tbsp. paprika
2 tbsp. cumin
2 tbsp. oregano
1 ½ tbsp. chili powder.
Red pepper, to taste
thyme (fresh)

directions:

1. cook onions, meat, bacon, and garlic together.
2. In a separate pot, combine tomatoes, canned tomatoes, celery, bell pepper, and beans. Let simmer for 30 minutes.
3. Add meat and bacon, corona, and ~~the~~ tequila. Then add all of the spices.
4. simmer for at least 2-3 hours. Garnish with sour cream and fresh cilantro, and serve.

Epilogue

And there you have it—my *la folie*, or crazy, forty. I have come a long way from the tiny boy who was born in a bakery in France—many years and halfway across the globe, to be precise. But if I close my eyes, it all feels like it took place only yesterday. My mother's smile, my father's hands, my grandmother's pigs, my grandfather's war stories, my sister's competitions, my friends at play—and right in the middle of it all, there was me.

My rebellious teenage years, my army days, my true love, my becoming a real man, my various businesses, the growth of my dear children—these have passed like the flash of the match that Damien used to light my father's oven. And woven into my life's tapestry has been hard work and change. During my forty years in the food industry, and even before, every bit of learning, every recipe, every taste, every joy, every mistake, every experience, good or bad, all of these have helped to write the story that is the essence of me. They have made me who I am.

You may have taken away a few bits of humor from my life's story, perhaps knowledge, or even a few recipes to make your own. But it is my hope that, above all of these, you recognize my dedication to food and, even more importantly, my love of my family. They fuel my heart and my soul.

My life has been far from perfect. I have always had great ambition, have orchestrated a great many successes, and have dealt with a few epic failures. The whole time, though, I have learned and grown—as a baker, as a husband and father, and as a human being. The New River Valley is quite different from the Loire Valley, where my story originated. But, in many ways, it is very similar. For wherever you have love and harvest, you have home. It is that simple, *n'est-ce pas?*

Every day, I awaken with a smile of gratitude. Current expansion into Salem, Virginia, and possibly beyond, bringing joy to the stomachs of my customers, creating edible works of art—these adventures fill my days. With my wife and children surrounding me, a wedding to plan, and a new grandson to spoil, I look forward to yet another *la folie* forty.

Acknowledgments

Thierry and I would be remiss if we did not thank:

Richard Thomas for his guidance and editing skills, Denise Baer for her editing, formatting, and cover wizardry, Danielle Tellier for reminding Thierry about all of the parts that he didn't remember, Chad Jones for his introduction, photography, and creative input, Franck and Aurore Tellier for their suggestions and consultation, Danielle Kessel for her artistic interpretation of Thierry's recipes, all of Thierry's customers over the last forty years— for their support and for allowing him the joy of creating lovely cuisine, and, last but not least, all of you who discover passion, knowledge, appreciation, and just the right amount of flavor within these pages. *Merci beaucoup!*

♦ ♦ ♦

Proceeds from the sale of this book will help support culinary students in the New River Valley. Thank you for your generosity.

About the Authors

Thierry Tellier is a pastry chef, husband, father, grandfather, and restaurateur who currently resides in the New River Valley of Virginia, where he owns and operates Our Daily Bread Bakery and Bistro. He was born in the Loire Valley of France, and has spent over forty years in the food industry. He is a multi-faceted creator of delicious cuisine, and his bakery-cafes have been recognized for their dedication to providing his local communities with palatable dishes laced with his signature French flair.

Thierry and his wife, Danielle, were both born a month apart in 1957, and her influence on him has been palpable, as the majority of their lives have been spent together. When not cooking, Thierry enjoys fishing, walking, snowshoeing, gardening, experiencing nature, antique collecting, and spending time with family and friends—all accompanied by his lovely wife. To learn more about Thierry, visit Our Daily Bread Bakery & Bistro's website: www.odbb.com.

Jennifer Jones doesn't just simply write. Writing is a part of who she is. She has been published in *The Best of Poetry Project 2014* from Fray'd Tag Publishing, the anthology *Silver Lining* from Baer Books Press, and the poetry anthology, *Crashing Waves*, from Swyers Publishing.

For more information, visit: www.wowjenwrites.net.

When not writing, Jennifer enjoys being a wife, mom, friend, foodie, and accidental coffee snob. She spends her limited free time reading, attending the theater, hanging out with her loved ones, cooking—especially the sweet stuff—and traveling. She currently resides with her husband, teenage daughter, and goofy dog in Christiansburg, Virginia.

49606908R00103

Made in the USA
Charleston, SC
28 November 2015